C

MARINA

THE PENALTY OF DEATH

Volume 102, Sage Library of Social Research

RECENT VOLUMES IN
SAGE LIBRARY OF SOCIAL RESEARCH

The PENALTY of DEATH

Thorsten Sellin

Volume 102
SAGE LIBRARY OF
SOCIAL RESEARCH

 SAGE PUBLICATIONS   Beverly Hills   London

For information address:

SAGE Publications, Inc.
275 South Beverly Drive
Beverly Hills, California 90212

SAGE Publications Ltd
28 Banner Street
London EC1Y 8QE, England

Printed in the United States of America

Library of Congress Cataloging in Publication Data
Main entry under title:

Sellin, Thorsten, 1896-
   The penalty of death.

   (Sage library of social research; v. 102)
   Bibliography: p.
   Includes index.
   1. Capital punishment. I. Title.
HV8694.S43   '364.6'6   80-203
ISBN 0-8039-1452-0
ISBN 0-8039-1453-9 pbk.

CONTENTS

PREFACE

The status of the death penalty in the United States of America today is anomalous. Although 36 of the 50 states have statutes which provide this punishment for one or more crimes, and hundreds of prisoners are confined in our state prisons under sentence of death, there have been only three executions since July 2, 1976, when the United States Supreme Court gave its approval to capital punishment laws that met certain specifications defined by the Court. This paradoxical situation illustrates the moral dilemma facing people in most of our states, who want laws that call for the death penalty for murder but, at the same time, are extremely reluctant to enforce them to the bitter end. Their support of capital punishment is chiefly rooted in beliefs in its deterrent power or in its appropriateness as an instrument of poetic justice. These beliefs will be examined in this book, as well as the difficulties facing the researcher who wants to know if they are reasonable.

One chapter has already been published. Chapter 5 is the English version of a lecture delivered January 24, 1979, at the Institut des Hautes Etudes de Belgique, Brussels, and published with the title "Intimidation générale et peine de mort" in the April 1979 issue of *Revue de Droit Pénal et de Criminologie* (Vol. 59, pp. 315-325).

I greatly appreciate the care with which Mrs Selma Pastor has typed the manuscript and prepared the index, and the assistance of Mrs Barbara Naab in procuring certain statistical data.

Gilmanton, New Hampshire   *Thorsten Sellin*

INTRODUCTION

The punishment prescribed by law for violators of its provisions is said to serve many different purposes. First, the suffering it inflicts on offenders satisfies the community's demand for what is called vengeance, retribution, retaliation, atonement, reprobation, or justice. Second, it may be regarded as a positive means of converting an offender into a consciously moral person. Third, it may make him law-abiding simply by causing him to fear what would happen to him if he were to commit a crime again. Fourth, it would serve as an object lesson to other potential law violators. Fifth, by depriving him of his life — or liberty — it would completely prevent — or temporarily or permanently curtail — his criminal activities. Nowadays, these aims are, respectively, called retribution, reformation, specific deterrence, general deterrence, and prevention. The supreme object of all measures taken to fulfill these aims is to achieve the protection of the community, i.e., its social institutions and the rights of its members, by reenforcing its moral code embodied in law and strengthening general respect for law and justice.

These views are deeply rooted. They were held by ancient lawgivers and philosophers of law. Retribution and general deterrence were the dominant aims of the laws of Moses and Draco, and they have remained so in the criminal law to the present time; but punishment was, of old, seen as serving other purposes as well. To Socrates "the object of all punishment which is rightly inflicted should be either to improve or benefit the subject or else make him an example to others, who will be deterred by the sight of his sufferings and reform their own conduct."[1] In his treatise, *The Laws*, Plato proposed that

> when anyone commits an act of injustice...the law will combine instruction and constraint, so that in the future either the criminal will never again dare to commit such a crime voluntarily, or he will do it a very great deal less often...This is something we can achieve only by laws of the highest quality. We may take action or simply talk to the criminal; we may grant him pleasures or make him suffer; we may honor him, we may disgrace him; we can fine him or give him gifts. We may use absolutely any means to make him hate injustice and embrace true justice — or at any rate not hate it. But suppose a lawgiver finds a man who is beyond cure — what legal penalty will he provide for this case? He will recognize that the best thing for all such people is to cease to live — best even for themselves. By passing on they will help others, too; first, they will constitute a warning against injustice, and secondly they will leave the state free of scoundrels. That is why the lawgiver should prescribe the death penalty in such cases by way of punishment for their crimes — but in no other case whatever.[2]

In his debate with Socrates, the Sophist Protagoras expressed the opinion that "he who desires to inflict rational punishment does not retaliate for a past wrong which cannot be undone; he has regard to the future and is desirous that the man who is punished and he who sees him punished may be deterred from doing wrong again. He punishes for the sake of prevention," but he who is wanting in justice and temperance and holiness and, in a word, manly justice, "must be taught

---

1. Plato, *Gorgias,* 525.
2. Plato, *The Laws,* 862-863. Seneca, in his essay *On Anger,* Chapter 5, accepted these views. "The law wants to correct [the offender] when it strikes, or improve others by the example, or give others more security by the supression of evil persons."

and punished until by punishment he becomes better, and he who rebels against instruction and punishment is either exiled or condemned to death under the idea that he is incurable."[3] Such views recur in one of the orations of Demosthenes. "There are two objects for which all laws are framed — to deter any man from doing what is wrong and, by punishing the transgressor, to make the rest better men."[4]

Although none of these ancient philosophers and orators quoted defined the chief purpose of punishment to be the enhancement of social solidarity and the toughening of the moral fiber of the community, they may well have had that in mind also. In modern times that purpose has been stressed by many thinkers. It was stated by Lecky, when he observed that "every system of law is a system of education, for it fixes in the mind of man certain conceptions of right and wrong, and of the proportionate enormity of different crimes,"[5] and to Emile Durkheim, sociologist, "punishment does not serve, or does it only secondarily, to correct the culprit or intimidate possible imitators. In either case, its effectiveness is certainly doubtful and, in any case, mediocre. Its true function is to maintain social cohesion intact by strengthening the vitality of the community's conscience." It is "above all destined to influence honest people; because it serves to heal the wounds inflicted on the feelings of a community; it cannot play this role except where such feelings exist and to the degree they have vitality."[6]

Among the punishments for crime, the death penalty is the only one that cannot be used to attain all the aims mentioned.

---

3. Irwin Edman, ed., *The Works of Plato* (New York: Modern Library, 1928), pp. 211-212.
4. Quoted in Donald Kagan, ed., *Sources in Greek Political Thought from Homer to Polybius* (New York: Free Press, 1965), p. 141.
5. W.E.H. Lecky, *History of European Morals from Augustus to Charlemagne,* 3rd. ed., rev., 2 vol. (New York: Appleton, 1924; reprint of 1869 ed.), vol. 2, p. 8.
6. Emile Durkheim, *De la division du travail social,* 4th ed. (Paris: Alcan, 1922; originally published in 1893), pp. 76-77.

Executing a criminal does not reform him,[7] nor can it deter him from committing a crime in the future. His death does effectively prevent him from continuing in a criminal career, but also deprives him of experiencing his punishment as a warning to desist from further criminal activity, which is the aim of specific deterrence. The only services to the community that the death penalty might be expected to perform are (1) the satisfaction of the demand for retribution by making the criminal pay for his misdeed with his life; (2) the realization of the hope that his execution will discourage others from committing capital crimes, i.e., general deterrence; and (3) the removal of the danger that his survival would pose to society, i.e., prevention.

Retribution strikes the offender. His execution cancels his debt to society. Accomplishing his death is an end in itself. If it satisfies the community's demand for retaliation more than would any other punishment, it is claimed to be morally justified. If this is a valid claim, no other defense of the death penalty is needed. For the believers in general deterrence, on the other hand, the offender is chiefly an instrument, a means to an end, the purpose of his execution being to cause people to fear his fate and therefore avoid committing capital crimes. If his execution produces this effect or truly protects the community from inevitable future danger to the lives of its members, its utilitarian value would alone suffice to justify its use.

The concept of retribution and those of general deterrence and prevention emerge from two different, unrelated, and

---

7. In spite of Schopenhauer, who viewed execution as a powerful instrument of salvation, "There can be no question whatever that the most hopeful means of working the reformation of a murderer, and by reformation I mean the conversion of his will from bad to good, is supplied by the certainty of his impending execution. When condemned criminals have entirely lost hope, they show actual goodness and purity in disposition, true abhorrence of committing any deed in the least degree bad or unkind; they forgive their enemies...and die gladly, peaceably and happily." Quoted by Ernest Bowen-Rowlands, *Judgement of Death* (London: W. Collins Sons, 1924), p. 137.

self-sufficient spheres of discourse, from each of which we can derive data revealing the force of the concepts and their consequences. Retribution is animated by feelings, the existence and force of which can be demonstrated, but which cannot be characterized as true or false. Utilitarian claims, however, can be tested; the truth or falsity of the assertions that the death penalty is a unique means of deterring people from committing capital crimes and protecting society can be determined by research. In subsequent pages, problems raised by these concepts will be examined, but their influence on the philosophy and theory of punishment in general will not be explored. Except for the first chapter, the discussion will be limited to the crime of murder. The research on general deterrence published in recent years, for instance, will not be discussed unless it has dealt with murder, murderers, and the penalty of death.

Chapter 1

THE DIVINE COMMAND:
DEATH TO THE WICKED

In debates on the legitimacy of capital punishment it is common to hear the Bible quoted by some speakers favoring or opposed to that penalty. The arguments will be found in later pages, but first we need to understand why beliefs that an Almighty God has ordered the extermination of some who have broken His commandments have survived.

Primitive man, faced with incomprehensible phenomena of nature and the dangers to which they exposed him, ascribed them to the activity of supernatural powers that controlled his fate and could favor or destroy his designs. Anyone whose conduct was looked upon as provoking the anger of these powers and thus inviting their wrath, which might strike not him alone but also his family and tribe, became a public enemy who had to be sacrificed to appease them. Thus sins against the deities became criminal acts endangering the community. Therefore, it is not surprising to find that the earliest codes of justice of which we have knowledge were assumed to have divine origin. So it was with the Law of Moses which has had a significant influence on the shaping of capital justice in the Western world.

After bringing his people "out of Egypt, out of the land of slavery," the Lord, according to the Bible, gave Moses on Mount Sinai the Ten Commandments or moral precepts which were to guide their conduct. They were to worship him alone, make no "wrong use of the name of the Lord, your God," keep the Sabbath day holy, honor their parents, commit no murder, adultery, or theft, give no false evidence against a neighbor or "covet your neighbor's house...your neighbor's wife, his slave, his slave-girl, his ox, his ass or anything that belongs to him" (Exod. 20:2-17; Deut. 5:7-21). The Lord promised to punish those who disobeyed His commandments. Before Moses died, he, as the Lord's agent, had communicated to Israel from time to time the specific sins which the Lord ordered expiated by the death of the offender.

Offenses against the faith and cult of Israel were treasonable "Whoever sacrifices to any god but the Lord shall be put to death" (Exod. 22:20).[1] The same punishment would strike "a prophet or dreamer...[who] offers you a sign or a portent and calls on you to follow other gods" (Deut. 13:1-5), the blasphemer (Lev. 24:13), the witch (Exod. 22:18), one who labored on the Sabbath day (Num. 15:32), one unqualified to come near to the Tabernacle (Num. 1:51; 18:7), and any relative or friend who "should entice you secretly to go and worship other gods" (Deut. 13:6).

The punishment of homicide revealed the survival of blood revenge or private vengeance in which criminal law is rooted. Long before the Mosaic era, the Lord had promised Noah that "he that sheds the blood of a man, for that man his blood shall be shed" (Gen. 9:6); but since Cain was not killed for slaying his brother Abel, but instead exiled and protected by a mark of the Lord against retaliation, intrafamily homicides were evidently treated differently. Originally, custom demanded a life for a life, whether a killing was inten-

---

1. All quotations are from *The New English Bible* (Oxford and Cambridge: University Presses, 1970).

tional or accidental, but a differentiation was already recognized in early Mosaic law and a device invented to effectuate it. "Whoever strikes another man and kills him shall be put to death. But if he did not act with intent, but they met by act of God, the slayer may flee to a place which I shall appoint for you" (Exod. 21:12ff).

There were to be three and ultimately six such cities of refuge "in which the homicide may take sanctuary. . . and his life shall be safe. Otherwise, when the dead man's next-of-kin who had the duty of vengeance pursued him in the heat of passion, he might overtake him, if the distance were great and take his life, although the homicide was not liable to the death penalty because there had been no previous enmity on his part" (Deut. 19:1-7). If one, who by treachery (Exod. 21:4) or ambush (Deut. 19:11ff) murdered someone and sought sanctuary in these places, "the elders of his own city shall send forth to fetch him; they shall hand him over to the next-of-kin and he shall die" (Deut. 19:11-13). The ancient custom of blood vengeance required that the execution of a murderer be performed by his own or his victim's nearest relative. If a man killed another with an iron or wooden instrument or a stone, "the dead man's next-of-kin shall put the murderer to death. . . . If the homicide sets upon a man openly of malice aforethought or aims a missile at him of set purpose and he dies, or if in enmity he falls upon him with his bare hands and he dies, then the assailant must be put to death; he is a murderer. His next-of-kin shall put the murderer to death" (Num. 35:16-21). No particular method of execution was prescribed.

It was forbidden to "accept payment for the life of a homicide guilty of a capital offense; he must be put to death" (Num. 35:32). The shedding of the blood of the murderer satisfied private vengeance and the community's need to cleanse itself of the sin of one of its members. "Expiation cannot be made on behalf of the land for the blood shed on it except by the blood of the man that shed it" (Num.

35:33-34). If a body was found in the open country and the slayer was unknown, the elders of the nearest town, whence it might be suspected that the murderer came, took a heifer to a stream in a ravine, killed it, and washed their hands over its body, solemnly declaring, "Our hands did not shed this blood, nor did we witness the bloodshed. Accept expiation, O Lord...and do not let the guilt of innocent blood rest upon the people Israel" (Deut. 21:1-9).

Justice was administered by tribal chiefs, elders, and priests and in case of murder "the homicide shall be put to death...only on the testimony of witnesses; the testimony of a single witness shall not be enough to bring him to his death" (Num. 35:30-31). Two or three witnesses were required to establish a charge that a capital "crime or sin" had been committed (Deut. 19:15), but upon conviction of murder, the execution of the offender was performed only by a member of the families concerned. In other capital offenses, however, private vengeance was excluded; the execution, usually by stoning, was a community affair. "Take the man who blasphemed out of the camp. Everyone who heard him shall put a hand on his head, and then all the community shall stone him to death" (Lev. 24:13-14). When a man was caught gathering sticks on the Sabbath day, the Lord said to Moses, "The man must be put to death; he must be stoned by all the community outside the camp" (Num. 15:32-36). If a relative or friend enticed a man to worship other gods, that man's "own hand shall be the first to be raised against him and then all the people shall follow. You shall stone him to death" (Deut. 13:6-10). A witch probably met the same fate (Exod. 22:18). "When a man has a son who is disobedient and out of control and will not obey his father or mother or pay attention when they punish him, then his father and mother shall...bring him" before the elders of the town and accuse him, and then "all the men of the town shall stone him to death" (Deut. 21:18-21). "Whoever strikes [or reviles] his father or mother" was undoubtedly punished in a similar manner (Exod. 21:15, 17; Lev. 20:9).

Sex offenses were also avenged by the community. "When a virgin is pledged in marriage to a man and another man comes to her in the town and lies with her, you shall bring both of them out to the gate of that town and stone them to death" (Deut. 22:23-24); but if the man rapes such a girl in the country, he alone will die (Deut. 22:25-26), the assumption being that in town the girl's cry for help would have been heard. Although the mode of execution was not specifically mentioned, other sex offenders presumably were killed by stoning too. "If a man commits adultery with his neighbor's wife, both...shall be put to death" (Lev. 20:10-11; Deut. 22:22). "Whoever has unnatural connection with a beast shall be put to death" (Exod. 22:19) "and you shall kill the beast" (Lev. 20:15-16). If a man had intercourse with his father's wife, his daughter-in-law, his uncle's wife or "with a man as with a woman," both partners should be executed (Lev. 20:11-20, 30). Should a man take "both a woman and her mother" all three should be burned (Lev. 20:14-15) and so should a priest's daughter who became a prostitute (Lev. 21:9). This was ancient custom, because when the patriarch Judah "was told that his daughter-in-law had behaved like a prostitute and through her wanton conduct was with child, Judah said, 'Bring her out so that she may be burnt' " (Gen. 38:24-25).

Kidnapping a man was also a capital crime (Exod. 21:15); in the last book of Moses it was noted that the victim had to be "a fellow-countryman, an Israelite," who had been treated harshly and sold by the kidnapper (Deut. 24:7).

In order to impress on people the heinousness of crime, the corpse of the person executed was to be gibbeted. "When a man is convicted of a capital offense and is put to death, you shall hang him on a gibbet; but his body shall not remain on the gibbet overnight; you shall bury it on the same day, for a hanged man is offensive (or accursed)'' (Deut. 21:22-23).[2]

It is not uncommon to find the invention of the *lex talionis* credited to Moses, i.e, the principle that the punishment of crime equal the offense. This practice was well illustrated in the Hammurabi code a thousand years earlier. It probably was introduced to limit the excesses of private vengeance, and it is defined in the Pentateuch. "Whenever hurt is done, you shall give life for life, eye for eye, tooth for tooth, hand for hand, foot for foot, burn for burn, bruise for bruise, wound for wound'' (Exod. 21:23-25; Lev. 24:19-20). The principle was followed also in the case of perjury. Giving false testimony should entail the same punishment that would have been inflicted on the accused if he had been convicted. "You shall show no mercy: life for life, eye for eye, tooth for tooth, hand for hand, foot for foot'' (Deut. 19:16-21).

One important provision shows that the Mosaic code did not permit private vengeance to blossom into a blood feud. "Fathers shall not be put to death for their children, nor children for their fathers; a man shall be put to death only for his own sin'' (Deut. 24:16).

The theocratic state founded by Moses would have a turbulent history during the next twelve centuries, but the letter of the capital laws would not change, because these laws were the command of Jehovah, the God of Israel. They lost, at last, all practical value when Augustus made Judea an imperial Roman province in 4 A.D., placed his procurator in charge of the country, and deprived the high court — the Sanhedrin — of the right to impose capital punishment; finally, Titus destroyed Jerusalem and its temple in 70 A.D., ending the Jewish state. Thenceforth, the Jewish people would live subject to the capital laws of their conquerors or of other states in which they found refuge until the Republic of Israel

---

2. "Every person found guilty of a capital offense and put to death had to be impaled on a stake." See *Encyclopedia Judaica* 5:142 (Jerusalem, 1971). Such impalement was practiced in Syria but not in Israel.

was constituted in 1948. Then, its parliament — the Knesset — abandoned the Mosaic law of a "life for a life" and abolished the death penalty in 1954 except for treason in wartime and for Nazi collaborators. When this move was contemplated four years earlier, a speaker in the Knesset argued that "it is said in the Torah that man was created in the image of God, and only by the command of God can his life be taken away from him. Our laws are not the command of God and therefore we have no right to take from a human his life, which is a gift of God" (Zorah Mannhaftig, July 24, 1950).

This aversion to the use of capital punishment was not a new phenomenon in Israel. A thousand years earlier it had nearly achieved its abolition by tactics quite familiar to the student of the history of Anglo-American criminal law. This is evident from legal doctrine and practice as early, at least, as two centuries before the fall of Jerusalem. "In crimes involving the death penalty the increased requirements as to the necessary witnesses and other evidence and the provision that the offender had to be warned of the penal consequences immediately before the commission of the crime virtually excluded the possibility of imposition of the death penalty."[3] That this aversion would persist in later centuries was only natural, considering the recurrent brutal persecutions the Jewish people would suffer for their faith.

A more formidable challenge to the merciless and stern justice of Moses than that offered by the reform-minded Hebrew jurists was to come from a religious Jewish cult based on the humane ethical tenets taught by Jesus of Nazareth, whose disciples saw in him the Messiah foretold by the ancient prophets. It seems evident from what we learn about

---

3. Asher Gulak, "[Law] Jewish," *Encyclopedia of the Social Sciences* 9:219-225; p. 223. "The Jewish jurists were opposed to the *lex talionis,* [but] they could not override the Biblical injunction and abrogate it completely by substituting another punishment in its stead. They nevertheless made every endeavor to so interpret the Biblical law and make the legal restrictions so numerous that it became almost impossible to impose a death sentence." Hyman E. Goldin, *Hebrew Criminal Law and Procedure* (New York: Twayne, 1952), p. 24.

Jesus from the Gospels that he was opposed to the use of capital punishment. Asked to approve the stoning of an adultress caught in the act, and knowing that the Law of Moses required that the witnesses to the offense begin the execution, he disarmed them by saying: "That one of you who is faultless shall throw the first stone" (John 7:53-58). He sent away the woman without condemning her, admonishing her to sin no more. Speaking to his disciples about the punishment of crime he said, "You have learned that they were told 'eye for eye, tooth for tooth.' But what I tell you is this, 'Do not set yourself against the man who wrongs you. If someone slaps you on the right cheek, turn and offer him your left' " (Matth. 5:38-39). Jesus preached brotherly love, mercy, and forgiveness, not retribution or retaliation, but his respect for civil authority as being ordained by God caused him to accept his own death sentence without protest. In the letter to the Romans, Paul reflected this attitude.

> Every person must submit to the supreme authorities. There is no authority but by act of God, and the existing authorities are instituted by Him; consequently anyone who rebels against authority is resisting a divine institution, and those who so resist have themselves to thank for the punishment they will receive. For government, a terror to crime, has no terrors for good behavior. You wish to have no fear of the authorities? Then continue to do right and you will have their approval, for they are God's agents working for your good. But if you are doing wrong, then you will have cause to fear them; it is not for nothing that they hold the power of the sword, for they are God's agents of punishment, for retribution on the offender. That is why you are obliged to submit. It is an obligation imposed not merely by fear of retribution but by conscience [Romans 13:1-6].

It should be noted that this admonition to the converts to the Christian faith to obey the laws of their temporal rulers did not contain an endorsement of any specific punishment im-

posed on violators and that the "sword" was the symbol and
not the instrument of justice.

As Christianity spread during the earliest centuries, its
adherents remained, in general, opposed to the death penalty. "Their simplicity," wrote Gibbon, "was offended by the
use of oaths; ...nor could their humane ignorance be con-
vinced that it was lawful on any occasion to shed the blood of
our fellow creatures, either by the sword of justice or by that
of war."[4] Among the early church fathers, "Tertullian
declared that a Christian could not impose the death penalty.
Origen claimed that a Christian, 'molded by Jesus,' would no
longer follow the law of Moses that ordained death for male-
factors. Lactantius wrote that even the opening of a capital
prosecution was not permitted. 'God's prohibition of killing
admits no exception.' "[5] Augustine's views were less consis-
tent. Pleading on behalf of some Donatist dissenters who had
murdered Christians, he wrote:

> We do not want to have the sufferings of the servants of God
> avenged by the infliction of precisely similar injuries in the
> way of retaliation. Not, of course, that we object to the
> removal from these wicked men of the liberty to perpetrate
> further crimes, but our desire is rather that justice be satisfied

---

4. Edward Gibbon, *The Decline and Fall of the Roman Empire*, 2 vol. (New York:
Modern Library, n.d.), vol. 1, p. 416 (originally published in 1776).

5. Paul Savey-Casard, *La peine de mort* (Geneva: Droz, 1968), p. 22. "The notion
of the sanctity of human life, which led the early Christians to combat and at last to
overthrow the gladiatorial games was carried by some of them to an extent
altogether irreconcilable with national independence and with the prevalent penal
system. Many of them taught that no Christian might lawfully take away life, either
as a soldier or by bringing a capital charge or by acting as an executioner.... The
thought that there is something impure and defiling, even in a just execution, is one
which may be traced through many ages, and executioners, as the ministers of the
law, have been from very ancient times regarded as unholy. In both Greece and
Rome the law compelled them to live outside the walls, and at Rhodes they were
never permitted even to enter the city." W.E.H. Lecky, *History of European Morals
from Augustus to Charlemagne*, 2 vol. (New York: Appleton, 1924), vol. 2, pp.
38-39.

without the taking of their lives or the maiming of their bodies in any particular; and that, by such coercive measures as may be in accordance with the laws, they be drawn away from their insane frenzy to the quietness of men in their sound judgment, or compelled to give up mischievous violence and betake themselves to some useful labour."[6]

But, "in the *City of God* (Book I, Chap. 21) he brushes away the argument derived from the prohibition of killing; this rule applies to persons acting solely on their own. God, master of life and death, has given the State 'by general commandment' the right to use the sword to safeguard public order. However, after acknowledging the duty of the Prince and judges to watch over the safety of all, Saint Augustine pronounces another duty equally imperious, the duty of pardon and mercy, which he bases squarely on the Gospel texts about the adultress."[7] The same texts led Ambrose to give the following reply to a secular judge who asked him if he had the right to impose a death sentence. " 'Consider what the law demands and mercy counsels. You are excused if you do it. You are praised if you don't.' "[8]

During the turbulent second and third centuries, when congregations of Christians were rapidly springing up among the peoples within the empire, Rome's tolerance of religions practiced by nations subservient to its rule did not extend to Christianity which was not, like Judaism, a national religion, but the beliefs of a heretical sect whose members were sporadically persecuted and even executed as enemies of the state. This may explain, in part, Tertullian's and Origen's attitudes to capital punishment. When Augustine and Ambrose wrote, the dogmas of the Christian church had already been formulated and in 325 A.D. adopted by the Council of

---

6. Quoted from his Epistles CLII and CLIII by Arthur Koestler, *Reflections on Hanging* (New York: Macmillan, 1957), p. 100.

7. Savey-Casard, *loc. cit.*

8. *Ibid.*, p. 23.

Nicaea, summoned by the Christian emperor Constantine, and in 380 A.D. Emperor Theodosius had decreed that "it is Our will that all the peoples who are ruled by the administration of Our Clemency shall practice that religion which the divine Peter the Apostle transmitted to the Romans" and that "those persons who follow this rule shall embrace the name of Catholic Christians. The rest, however, whom we adjudge demented or insane, shall sustain the infamy of heretical dogmas, their meeting places shall not receive the names of churches, and they shall be smitten first by divine vengeance and secondly by the retribution of Our own initiative, which we shall assume in accordance with the divine judgment."[9] Thenceforth, Catholic countries, regarding heresy as a crime against the state, would suppress it by various means, including the penalty of death. The Church would develop its own judicial system and a canon law that threatened heretics and other sinners with penance and excommunication, but "in general the ecclesiastical tribunals did not make use of either death or mutilation as punishments; nor did they permit corporal punishments which would result in loss of blood."[10] This suggests that the early Christian aversion to the death penalty remained dominant, but it did not prevent the Church from taking advantage of that penalty found in the law of secular states. In the face of the enormous spread of heretical sects in the twelfth and thirteenth centuries,[11] the traditional procedures of the ecclesiastical courts in dealing with heresy broke down. In 1230, Gregory IX created special papal inquisitorial courts, untrammeled by the restrictions of the canon law, and in 1252, Innocent IV authorized the inquisitors to use torture to

---

9. *The Theodosian Code*...A Translation...by Clyde Pharr, 16:2. (Princeton, NJ: Princeton University Press, 1952).

10. H. D. Hazeltine, "Cannon Law," *Encyclopedia of the Social Sciences* 3:179-185; p. 183.

11. Walter Wakefield and Austin P. Evans, *Heresies of the High Middle Ages* (New York: Columbia University Press, 1969).

extract confessions. "Princes and magistrates were...commanded by the Church (under pain of excommunication, confiscation and deposition) to execute the sentences of these...papal *inquisitores*[12] and "civil governments were induced to stiffen their laws in defense of the orthodox faith.... As a consequence death by burning came to be prescribed for heretics in most states before the end of the thirteenth century."[13] The English parliament did so in 1401. The inquisitors, having convicted a person of heresy, handed him over to secular justice to suffer death.

> In abandoning heretics to the secular arm, they besought the State officials to act with moderation, and avoid 'all bloodshed and all danger of death.' This was unfortunately an empty formula which deceived no one. It was intended to safeguard the principle which the Church had taken for her motto: *Ecclesia abhorret sanguine.* In strongly asserting this traditional law, the Inquisitors imagined that they thereby freed themselves from all responsibility, and kept from imbruing their hands in bloodshed. We must take this for what it is worth. It has been styled 'cunning' and 'hypocrisy'; let us call it simply a legal fiction."[14]

This practice might appear either as the endorsement of capital punishment by the Church or merely as its recognition of the duty of Christians to submit to the laws of civil authorities, as Paul had taught. The latter is consonant with the opposition to the death penalty revealed in the New Testament which in this respect departed from the stern justice defined in the laws of Moses. These laws had not been completely ignored by secular authorities, as is evident from some of the legislation of the Christian emperors of Rome

---

12. G. G. Coulton, *Medieval Panorama* (Cambridge: University Press, 1938), p. 471.
13. Carl Stephenson and Bryce Lyon, *Medieval History,* 4th ed. (New York: Harper & Row, 1962), p. 427.
14. Coulton, *op. cit.,* p. 474, quoting Abbé Vacandard.

and later rulers, but their full force as the laws of God that should be the laws of the land would not be felt in some nations until an event occurred which would split the Church. That event was the Protestant Reformation.

The Protestant Reformation, sparked in 1517 by the Augustinian friar Martin Luther (1483-1546) when he challenged the Church's sale of indulgences, was a complex movement. "Politically," writes Hearnshaw,

> it was a revolt of the Teuton against Latin domination, and also a rebellion of princes and cities against Imperial control; socially, it was a rising of the oppressed against their lords, ecclesiastical and civil; economically, it was a secularist assault upon the accumulated wealth of the Church; ecclesiastically, it was an insurrection of the laity against the clergy; morally, it was a protest against the degeneracy of the priesthood and the flagrant separation of religion from ethics; theologically, it was a return to the New Testament, to personal piety and to the simplicity of the doctrine of justification by faith; intellectually, it was a revolt of the individual against authority and a reassertion of the right of freedom of speech."[15]

In the countries which subscribed to the new religion, its influence on penal legislation was significant. Both Luther and especially John Calvin (1509-1564), leaders of the two most important Protestant churches, found in the ancient laws of Moses a guide to human conduct and the punishment of transgressors of God's ordinances, a *lex divina positiva* bind-

---

15. F.J.C. Hearnshaw, ed., *The Social and Political Ideas of Some Great Thinkers of the Renaissance and the Reformation* (New York: Barnes and Noble, 1967), p. 28.

ing on all Christian peoples. This doctrine would lead to a great expansion of the role of capital punishment, as states began to transform some offenses previously under the jurisdiction of ecclesiastical courts into felonies punishable by the state. Two illustrations of this phenomenon will suffice — the impact of Lutheranism on the development of Swedish law and Calvinism on the Puritan legislation of New England.

Sweden[16]

Sweden abandoned Catholicism, partly due to the inspiring sermons of Olavus Petri, a friar who had been Luther's student at the University of Wittenberg, and partly because the king, Gustavus Vasa, needed the revenues which the bishops and monasteries gained from their extensive holdings; they owned about one-fifth of the realm, untaxed. The reformation was promptly reflected in penal legislation. The reception of the retributive Mosaic laws was foreshadowed in a statute of 1563 which made certain offenses, previously punished with penances and fines imposed by ecclesiastical courts, into felonies punished capitally. The preamble of the statute explained that this was in accord with the divine command and that "since many plagues — pestilence, famine, inflation and other ills — are visited on humans because of their sins, so that for one man's sin an entire kingdom often must suffer and be punished, God's anger must be prevented and such criminals not spared for the sake of money, considering that evil and malice are thus not lessened and those who practice them given more reason and frequent opportunities to provoke God." The god who was to be propitiated

---

16. In this section are summaries, at times verbatim, of appropriate parts of the fine survey of the history of the Swedish penal system in Gustav Olin's "Nagra blad ur det svenska straffsystemets historia," in *Minnesskrift ägnad 1734 ars lag,* 3 vol. (Stockholm: Marcus, 1934), vol. 2, pp. 807-863.

was the god of Israel who rained sulphur and fire on the land when angered. The official sanction of the reception was given in a royal decree of 1608 which ruled that in the case of certain crimes, "courts should apply God's law as stated in the Scriptures." To aid the judges in meeting this directive, a compilation of the appropriate dicta of the Pentateuch was printed as an appendix to the penal code. Thus penal laws "designed two thousand years earlier for mideastern tribes of primitive culture became the law of Sweden in the 1600s."

This biblical justice, binding on the courts, expanded the domain of capital punishment, but it was to be modified considerably by the appellate courts and the royal prerogative of mercy, at least during the first half of the seventeenth century. Those convicted of the most serious crimes — treason, blasphemy, murder, rape, incest, and bestiality, for instance — were unpardonable and could be executed forthwith; but other capital cases had to be reviewed by the appellate courts and finally by the king. Capital sentences for infanticide, aggravated assault — even on parents — adultery, and bigamy were often commuted to a fine or imprisonment at hard labor.[17] This mitigating development would slacken during the last half of the century when the Lutheran orthodoxy became most firmly entrenched and the Mosaic law more literally enforced. When, in 1699 for instance, the court of appeals commuted the death sentence of a woman, who had slightly assaulted her mother, to a fine of one hundred dalers in silver and public penance, the king ordered her execution "since the Holy Writ clearly and expressly stated that those who assault their parents cannot and should not be spared." As late as 1706, the king, refusing to accept a judgment of the court of appeals, ordered a male atheist who had blasphemed and mocked the sacraments to be executed, his right hand

---

17. The nature of this punishment and the conditions of the prisons may be inferred from the motivation for commuting one sentence; it was noted that "1½ years of prison was equivalent to a death penalty" (Olin, *op. cit.,* p. 825).

first cut off and his tongue excised, and then to be decapitated, his head and body burned, and his hand and tongue nailed to the pillory on the market square. He had translated a German book considered atheistic, had made irreverent remarks about the sacraments, and had called the pastors heretics. A few years earlier, two bosuns had been decapitated and burned because in singing a hymn in church they had changed the word Jesus to Satan in the verse "I have Jesus in my heart." The reverence for the ancient laws of Israel, which contained the word of God, even caused learned jurists to question the power of an absolute monarch to modify them.

Among the sex offenses, bestiality — i.e., sexual intercourse with an animal — seems to have been more abhorred by people than was homosexuality, which was ignored by Christopher's Law of the Realm (1442). It was made punishable like bestiality with decapitation and burning in 1713, but in practice was given lesser punishments. Most of those convicted of bestiality were adolescent cowherds, which moved the king, in 1686, to urge the provincial governors to make the peasants employ women in that occupation. Finally, the code of 1734 expressly ordered that "for herding, females shall be used, when possible, and not boys, on pain of a fine of ten dalers." The warning was not heeded. "No fewer than 151 persons were executed for bestiality during the period 1751-1778, most of them male youths in the seventeen to twenty age group."[18]

The influence of the Mosaic law on Swedish justice would remain for a long time. The penal code of 1734 provided the death penalty for 68 crimes, among them murder, treason, blasphemy, lese majesty, certain cases of adultery, incest, rape, bigamy, bestiality, armed disturbances of church services, and witchcraft causing injury to person or property. Striking parents, however, was no longer punishable by

18. Lars Levander, *Brottsling och bödel* (Stockholm: Åhlen & Söners Förlag, 1933), p. 100.

death; another Mosaic punishment was substituted — 40 lashes.[19]

The 1734 code was adopted at the dawn of the great century of Enlightenment, the effect of which would become evident in the epoch-making royal ordinance of 1779 which largely repudiated biblical notions and abolished the death penalty for witchcraft, some sex offenses, and so on. In the code of 1864, the death penalty was retained only for treason and various kinds of homicide. The Mosaic demand of "a life for a life" finally disappeared from the Swedish penal code in 1921.

From Geneva to New England

"In the seventeenth century," wrote Beard, "the Old Testament, the Mosaic legislation, the Jewish kingdom and church assumed a place in religious thought and practice to which the earlier history of Christianity offers little that is like."[20] The best example is the theocratic state which the Protestant reformer John Calvin founded in Geneva, Switzerland, in 1541. Calvin, jurist and theologian, "believed that all Scripture was written under the direct dictation of the Holy Spirit and was to be received by the church as a living voice of Heaven."[21] For him the Decalogue defined all crimes and the laws of Moses defined the punishment, usually death, for their perpetrators. The result was a "holy reign of terror, which Calvin established and left behind him as a legacy to Geneva," characterized by "first, the vast extension given to the idea of crime, and next, the worse than Draconian severity of the punishments inflicted. Adultery was repeatedly punished by death. A child was beheaded for having struck

19. The Bible does not mention the manner of flogging. Talmudic law reduced the number of lashes to 39. *Encyclopedia Judaica* 6:1348.
20. Rev. Charles Beard, *The Reformation of the 16th Century* (Ann Arbor: University of Michigan Press, 1962; originally published 1883), p. 259.
21. *Ibid.*, p. 258.

father and mother...in some cases drowning [was] inflicted
for unchastity.''[22] The burning alive of the "blasphemer"
Servetus, a dissident unitarian, in 1553, became a cause
célèbre. On the other hand, the strict adherence of Calvinistic
theologians to the commands of the Bible led them to oppose
the custom of hanging thieves since it was not prescribed by
Moses. Eventually this would have a significant influence on
the movement to establish houses of correction.[23] They were
equally opposed to the commonly used judicial torture for
which they could find no biblical sanction.[24]

Lutheranism had become a state religion in northern Ger-
many and the Scandinavian countries by the end of the sixteenth century. Its influence was felt in England too, for in
1526, William Tyndale, who had visited Luther in Wittenberg, published his translation of the New Testament,
followed in 1530 by his rendition of the Pentateuch into
English. Four years later, Miles Coverdale's translation of the
Bible appeared; like Luther, he was a converted Augustinian
friar.[25] The full extent of the Old Testament's stern justice
now became known to all literate persons who had been
unable to read Latin. The power of the divine command was
soon reflected in legislation. In 1533, "unnatural offences"
were made felonies by statute, as were conjuration, witchcraft, sorcery, and enchantment in 1541 and bigamy in 1603.
These had previously been ecclesiastical offenses punished by
penances and excommunication.[26] Gradually the Protestant
conception of the basis for capital justice won acceptance.

---

22. *Ibid.*, pp. 259-260.
23. Thorsten Sellin, *Pioneering in Penology: The Amsterdam Houses of Correction
in the Sixteenth and Seventeenth Centuries* (Philadelphia: University of Pennsylvania Press, 1944), pp. 17, 25-26.
24. Hellmuth von Weber, *Calvinismus und Strafrecht,* undated reprint from
Festschrift fuer Eberhard Schmidt, pp. 39-53.
25. A. G. Dickens, *The English Reformation* (New York: Schocken, 1964), pp. 71,
130.
26. James Fitzjames Stephen, *A History of the Criminal Law of England,* 3 vol.
(London: Macmillan, 1885), vol. 2, p. 207.

"In the sixteenth and seventeenth century," writes a leading historian of law, "it would have required considerable audacity on the part of any lawyer to deny that the only ultimate, supreme authority lay in a law higher than any man-made ordinance — the eternal dictates of natural justice, reason, or equity; or, in its theological aspect, the law of God."[27] This was truth eternal to the followers of Calvin, and among them of the many leading English clergymen who sought sanctuary in Geneva and Strassburg during the reign of Mary, who attempted to restore the power of the Catholic Church in England and sent many Protestant "heretics" to the stake. Upon her death and the accession of Elizabeth to the throne, the emigrés

> returned to their native land, fired with the spirit of the crusaders, to spread the gospel of Calvinism. In ardent sermons they warned the people that God had chosen His own from the mass of those predestined to damnation, that He would not tolerate the breach of His Commandments, that His delight was a contrite soul rather than church ornaments and ceremonials, that the one sure guide for the State as well as for the individual was the Bible, that the civil government, while separate from the Church, should be in the hands of godly men, who could give religion their hearty support and suppress error.... They demanded the 'completion' of the Reformation. By this they meant the acceptance by the established Church of all of Calvin's doctrines, the abolition of ceremonial in worship, and the ousting from their cures of clergymen who were not in accord with their views.[28]

To the English Calvinists, who became known as Puritans,

---

27. C. K. Allen, *Law in the Making,* 7th ed. (Oxford: Clarendon Press, 1964), p. 446.
28. Thomas Jefferson Wertenbaker, *The Puritan Oligarchy* (New York: Scribner's, 1947), pp. 18-19. The "established Church" was the Anglican Church whose creed was largely Lutheran and which had retained the hierarchical organization and much of the ritual of the Catholic Church from which it was divorced by Henry VIII.

a church did not mean anything like the Anglican Church
with its clergy, bishops, and archbishops, appointed or approved by the king, and communicants owing allegiance to
these masters. To them "any company of true believers
associating themselves together would constitute a Church of
Christ by making a solemn covenant with God and with each
other." Each such "church" would be autonomous, electing
its own pastor, teacher, elders, and other officers and acting
together, democratically, on issues confronting it. A sentiment of brotherhood would be fathered by having delegates
from such congregations meet in synods to discuss common
problems. Some leaders of the sect, distrustful of democracy,
held that the government of a congregation should be vested
in the pastor, teacher, and elders who should make sure that
"the ordinances of God be 'truly taught and practiced' and
that the people obey 'willingly and readily.' "[29] These were
revolutionary ideas. They brought harassment and even
persecution on the Puritans, and some were driven into exile
and some executed. Finally, some of them were determined to
leave England and establish their church elsewhere, on the
pattern of Geneva which John Knox, the Scottish
Presbyterian leader, had called "the most perfect school of
Christ that ever was in the earth since the days of the
Apostles."[30] They chose New England.

The first settlement was made in 1620 at Plymouth by a
group later called Pilgrims. The colony was absorbed in 1691
by the larger and more prosperous Massachusetts Bay Colony
which had begun to settle the area around Boston in 1630,
but during their independence the Pilgrims prescribed the
death penalty for treason, murder, witchcraft, adultery, rape,
sodomy, and arson, although they actually applied it only to
three murderers and one sodomist. It remained for the
Puritans of the Bay Colony to adopt a more comprehensive

29. *Ibid.,* pp. 19-21.
30. Dickens, *op. cit.,* p. 198.

code of the capital laws of Moses to be enforced by civil magistrates who must be devout members of the church. In 1636, John Cotton prepared a model code, "Moses, his Judicials." It was not enacted into law, but "its heavy reliance upon Scripture provides an important illustration of the strong religious influence which infused Puritan thinking about law and the administration of justice.... Pursuant to literal texts of the Old Testament, the death penalty was prescribed for blasphemy, idolatry, witchcraft, false worship, sabbath breaking, murder, adultery, incest, sodomy, bestiality, man stealing, false witness, reviling the magistrates, cursing or smiting of parents."[31] In 1641, the legislature — the General Court — adopted a code known as the Body of Liberties which included Cotton's capital crimes except the offenses of false worship, Sabbath breaking, incest, reviling magistrates, and cursing or smiting parents. The definitions of the crimes were taken nearly verbatim from the Old Testament with explicit references to the specific biblical texts mandating the death penalty.[32] Two years later, rape was added to the list and in 1647 cursing or smiting a parent or being a rebellious son was also added, if the offender was over fifteen years of age. A second offense of denying that Scripture was the Word of God — heresy — was made capital in 1648. So was the return to the colony of a Jesuit after having been banished, a provision extended to Quakers in 1661.[33] The "rebellious son" provision was repealed in 1672.

The Court of Assistants showed considerable restraint in the administration of these statutes, aided by the biblical injunction requiring that two or three witnesses to the crime be

---

31. George Lee Haskins, *Law and Authority in Early Massachusetts* (New York: Macmillan, 1960), p. 125.
32. Richard C. Donnelly, Joseph Goldstein, and Richard Schwartz, *Criminal Law* (Glencoe, II: Free Press, 1962), p. 310; Edwin Powers, *Crime and Punishment in Early Massachusetts, 1620-1692* (Boston: Beacon Press, 1966), pp. 544-546.
33. The Puritan intolerance of dissenters was shown most glaringly in their persecution of the Quakers in 1659-1666; four of these "hereticks" were hanged.

produced. During 1630-1640, the three death sentences passed were for murder, and during the last ten years before the
charter of the colony was revoked in 1684, nine persons
received death sentences for murder, one for rape, and one
for sodomy, while of four persons condemned for adultery,
two were whipped and two only exposed at the gallows.[34]
Such moderation would not be shown the Salem "witches"
in 1691-1692. Their trial resulted in the hanging of fourteen
women and five men and the pressing of one man to death,
all in obedience to the divine command that no witch be
allowed to live. The episode signaled the coming end of the
Mosaic laws of the "Bible Commonwealth." The Bay Colony became a Royal Province and, in 1692, the General
Court reenacted the earlier laws, but the Privy Council
repealed them three years later because witchcraft,
blasphemy, and incest had been made punishable by death.
Among the capital crimes redefined the following year by the
General Court, treason, murder, sodomy, rape, and
polygamy still bore a Mosaic stamp which would not be eras-
ed until the establishment of the Commonwealth in 1780. The
death penalty for polygamy was abolished in 1784, for
sodomy in 1805, and for treason, rape, and arson in 1852,
leaving murder as the only capital crime in Massachusetts.
This last vestige of the retributive and retaliatory Mosaic
legislation finally disappeared in 1975 after two decades of
disuse by courts and executives deaf to the divine command
of "life for life."[35]

The Command Muted

Today, the divine command is muted and no longer heeded

---

34. Powers, *op. cit.,* pp. 407-408.
35. *Commonwealth* v. *O'Neal*, 339 NE, 2d 676 (Mass. 1975). The Puritan laws of
Moses were also adopted by the Connecticut and New Haven colonies in 1642, in
East Jersey in 1668, and by New Hampshire in 1679. They figure prominently in the
Duke of York's laws of 1676.

by the faithful, with one exception. When a life has been feloniously taken, they deem the murderer's life forfeited in retaliation — "life for life" — even though this purpose may be disguised in their rhetoric. God's command, objectified in the Ten Commandments and the Mosaic laws, is subjected to analysis designed to elicit what God really meant. In the process, both the Old and the New Testaments are appealed to. The Decalogue in the former and the ethic of love propounded in the Gospels are interpreted as serving only as moral precepts for individuals, while the Moasic legislation is said to be a guide to what the state should punish in the name of God, and Paul's directives to the Romans an endorsement of magistrates as "God's agents" who "hold the power of the sword." In other words, the Decalogue declares that murder is a sin, the Law of Moses prescribes its consequence as ordained by God, and Paul sanctifies executions. This argument, variously phrased and buttressed by citations to scriptural texts, is still occasionally heard in legislative halls or used by some witness during legislative hearings on bills calling for the abolition of capital punishment. Its most moderate formulation is exemplified in the minority opinion appended to a report issued in 1959 by a Massachusetts commission. "Only God," it states, "who created human life has the right to take it away. Since, however, the authority of the State derives ultimately from God, and is exercised in God's name, it is not inconsistent to hold that the State may claim the right, in the name of God, to take away human life in circumstances in which this would appear clearly to be in accord with God's own will." But, continues the report, this right can be claimed only

> when it can be shown to be a necessary means for protecting society against criminal attack, which endangers its very foundations....In this area of its thinking, the State is not concerned with problems of vengeance and hatred on the one hand, nor of rehabilitation, treatment or parole on the other.

Its main and all-important objective is what measure will best serve as a deterrent to would-be assassins and as a protection to all its members. . . The inflicting of capital punishment can be justified only if it serves as a deterrent in relation to future possible crimes of the same order, and only if less drastic measures towards the same end will not be sufficiently effective.[36]

This arrogant imposition of a limit on God's authority means that action by the state "in accord with God's own will" should be taken only as a last resort when something more "effective" cannot be devised. Such views would surely have been declared heretical by the Puritans.

History shows that the power of the divine command to determine the punishment for crime has largely eroded; but retribution, which the laws of Moses visited upon offenders, is still the dominant aim of capital laws. "Several writers," wrote Edward Westermarck,

maintain that the statements in the Bible, which command capital punishment, have an obligatory power on all Christian legislators; we even meet with the assertion that the object of this punishment is not the protection of civil society, but to carry out the justice of God, in whose name "the judge should sentence and the executioner strike." But I venture to believe that the chief motive for retaining the punishment of death in modern legislation is the strong hold which the principle of talion has on the minds of legislators, as well as on the mind of the public. This supposition derives much support from the fact that capital punishment is popular only in the case of murder. "Blood, it is said, will have blood, and the imagination is flattered with the notion of the similarity of the

---

36. *Report. . .of the Special Commission. . .Investigating. . .the Abolition of the Death Penalty. . .*(Boston: Commonwealth of Massachusetts, House, No. 2575, 1959), pp. 65-67. One of the two signers was the Most Reverend Thomas J. Riley, Auxiliary Roman Catholic Bishop of Boston.

suffering produced by the punishment with that inflicted by the criminal.' ''[37]

37. Edward Westermarck, *The Origin and Development of Moral Ideas,* 2nd ed. 2 vol. (London: Macmillan, 1912), vol. 1, p. 496.

Chapter 2

RETRIBUTION:
SUCCESS OR FAILURE?

The punishment of a criminal can be looked upon as a retributive or retaliatory social reaction to the evil he has caused. Capital punishment, wrote Montesquieu,

> represents a kind of retaliation, by which society withdraws protection from a citizen who has sought to destroy another citizen. This punishment is derived from the nature of the crime, drawn from the fund of Reason and the springs of Good and Evil. A citizen deserves death, when he has violated the security of another and has gone so far as to kill him or attempt to kill him. The death penalty thus employed may be described as the medicine for a social malady.

And Immanuel Kant, echoing the Old Testament, proclaimed that "whoever has committed *murder* must die.... . Even if a municipal society unanimously agreed to dissolve itself... the last murderer lying in its jail ought to be executed before implementation of the agreement... in order that everyone might receive his desert."[2]

---

1. *De l'esprit des loix* (1748), Book 12, Chap. 4.
2. James Heath, *Eighteenth Century Penal Theory* (London: Oxford University Press, 1963), p. 273, quoting from Kant's *Metaphysics of Morals* (1796).

Such categorical demands for revenge or retribution are still heard, though they are generally couched in demands for "justice." However, advocates of this penal policy also usually claim that the death penalty is a deterrent or a preventive or serves to promote social solidarity. Many seem to subscribe to the views of the learned Victorian legal historian, Sir James Fitzjames Stephen, who wrote:

> In cases which outrage the moral feelings of the community to a great degree, the feeling of indignation and desire for revenge, which is excited in the minds of decent people, is, I think, deserving a legitimate satisfaction. If a man commits a brutal murder, or if he does his best to do so and fails only by accident...I think [he] should be destroyed, partly in order to gratify the indignation which such crimes produce...and partly in order to make the world wholesomer than it would otherwise be by ridding it of people as much misplaced in civilized society as wolves or tigers would be in a populous country.[3]

Furthermore, "the infliction of punishment by law gives definite expression and a solemn ratification and justification to the hatred which is excited by the commission of the offense, and which constitutes the moral or popular as distinguished from the conscientious sanction of that part of that morality which is also sanctioned by the criminal law. The criminal law thus proceeds upon the principle that it is morally right to hate criminals, and it confirms and justifies that sentiment by inflicting upon criminals punishments which express it."[4]

That the criminal law is rooted in popular feelings of revenge has been asserted by other scholars. "Modern criminal justice," wrote Makarewicz, "retains popular

---

3. James Fitzjames Stephen, *A History of the Criminal Law of England,* 3 vol. (London: Macmillan, 1883), vol. 1, p. 478.
4. *Ibid.,* vol. 2, p. 81.

vengeance as its fundamental point of departure. Modern punishment, like that of primitive peoples, is a *vindicta publica*. The retribution on which it is based is nothing but vengeance, although it is gradually gaining in objectivity and practicality. The slogan of the future, the 'ideal' of punishment, seems to be that vengeance shall be exacted only when it can be socially useful."[5] For Durkheim, "punishment remains, at least in part, an act of vengeance. People say that we do not make a culprit suffer for the purpose of making him suffer, but it is nevertheless true that we find it just that he suffer.... . This expression of public vindictiveness, which continuously recurs in the language of the courts, is no vain word."[6]

Today, where death is threatened or inflicted as punishment for murder, it is basically the feeling that a murderer should pay for his misdeed with his life that inspires and sustains capital legislation. It finds expression in popular polls, legislative enactments, judicial opinions, and stridently in media of mass communication, when some particularly brutal crime has been committed. Its existence was recognized by the British Royal Commission on Capital Punishment, when it noted in its report of 1953 that "there is a strong and widespread demand for retribution in the sense of reprobation — not always unmixed in the popular mind with that of atonement and expiation" (Par. 53), and in 1976, Justice Stewart of the United States Supreme Court said that "the instinct for retribution is part of the nature of man.... . Indeed, the decision that capital punishment may be the appropriate sanction in extreme cases is an expression of the community's belief that certain crimes are themselves so grievous an affront to humanity that the only adequate response may be the penalty of death." He feared that

---

5. J. Makarewicz, *Einfuehrung in die Philosophie des Strafrechts auf entwicklungsgeschichtlicher Grundlage* (Stuttgart: Enke, 1906), p. 271.
6. Emile Durkheim, *De la division du travail social,* (Paris: Felix Alcan, 1922), p. 55.

"when people begin to believe that organized society is unwilling or unable to impose upon criminal offenders the punishment they 'deserve,' then there are sown the seeds of anarchy — of self-help, vigilante justice and lynch law."[7] The fact that 35 legislatures and Congress had reenacted the death penalty seemed to Justice White to refute "any claim that life imprisonment is adequate punishment to satisfy the need for reprobation and retribution."[8] In reaffirming the constitutionality of the death penalty, which the Court had all but outlawed four years earlier (*Furman* v. *Georgia*), retribution must have been the dominant spur, since the Court rejected all empirical evidence concerning the effectiveness of capital punishment in protecting society.

In May 1976, the Canadian Parliament debated the issue of capital punishment ending with a vote of total abolition. During the debate, several speakers defended the penalty as the only just and fitting one for murder. "Human life is sacred and...its sacredness must be enforced by depriving of life anyone who deprives another person of life." "The death penalty should be imposed on a murderer because it is the severest form of retribution for the severest form of offense." "Since the crime that takes a life is irrevocable, so must be punishment." "The ultimate justification of punishment is...that it is the emphatic denunciation by the community of a crime, and from this point of view there are some murders which demand the most emphatic denunciation of all, namely the death penalty." One abolitionist speaker, who believed that "we need retribution against murderers for the sake of the safety and cohesiveness of society," did not think that this necessarily required the death penalty. Another thought that "all the retentionist arguments...are reminiscent of revenge," and one noted that "revenge...is an opinion held by many people; they equate revenge with justice.

---

7. *Gregg* v. *Georgia,* July 2, 1976.
8. *Roberts* v. *Louisiana,* July 2, 1976.

A high percentage of the mail I have received merely supports
capital punishment on this basis.''[9]

This sample of opinions indicates that in the infliction of
the death penalty on murderers, retribution in its pure form
or as a dominant ingredient rules where this penalty is sanctioned by law. Even in abolitionist countries the spirit of
retribution may revive due to special circumstances. After the
last world war a wave of retaliation swept over the abolitionist countries of Europe that had been occupied by the
German military forces — Belgium, the Netherlands, Den-
mark, Norway — leading to the trial and execution of
thousands of collaborators with the enemy. Occasional polls
of public opinion in abolitionist states today show that sentiments favoring the death penalty are still strong. We must,
therefore, reckon with this view of the purpose of capital
justice, adherents of which see in the execution of the
murderer the fulfillment of what justice and morality demand. Their opponents maintain, with equal fervor, that execution by the state is as reprehensible as murder and morally
wrong. The issue belongs in the spheres of metaphysics and
moral philosophy. It incites emotional debates that pit people
of conflicting faiths against one another. Such conflicts cannot be resolved by reason but only by the success of one side
in converting the other to its faith. As Stephen said (vol. 2,
p. 91), ''It is useless to argue upon questions of sentiment.
All that any one can do is to avow the sentiments which he
holds and denounce those which he dislikes.''

If retributive justice absolutely required that murderers be
put to death, logic would compel us to assume, with Immanuel Kant, that everyone who deliberately takes the life of
another should be executed, without discrimination. Even the
strictest retributionist would exempt from this rule children,
the insane, and those who commit excusable or justifiable

---

9. *House of Commons Debates,* vol. 119, pp. 13239, 13376, 13405, 13541, 13628,
13867, 14489.

homicides, but this would still leave most killers to face the executioner. Actually, nothing like that happens. Even the most ardent believer in the dogma of "a life for a life," who examines the facts of how capital justice actually works, would have to concede that the dogma is an illusion. A look at some facts will show the truth of this assertion.

First of all we note that most criminal homicides are no longer subject to the law of talion. None of our laws requires that those guilty of willful or negligent manslaughter be put to death, nor do we require that all murderers suffer this penalty. That punishment is now reserved for those committing capital murder, usually called murder in the first degree. This designation is given to two distinct and psychologically different classes of criminal homicide. The first class contains "deliberate, malicious, premeditated" killings. In the second class we find homicides incidentally done or caused by someone while committing a felony. The first statute defining such felony-murders was adopted by Pennsylvania in 1794, when a person was declared guilty of murder in the first degree if he caused someone's death while committing arson, rape, robbery, or burglary. Today, the death penalty laws of the states retain both classes but do not always define them uniformly, especially in the case of felony-murder. Finally, a person is guilty of capital murder, even though he did not personally kill anybody but did participate as an accomplice in the crime or in the crime which led to the killing.

Since we wish to know how many persons guilty of capital murder receive their "just deserts", we must first determine how many capital murderers there are in the population of a death penalty state and then find out what happens to them. That determination depends in part on what population is potentially able to commit capital murder. In most states this means all sane persons above a certain age, but in Rhode Island it means convicts "committed to confinement to the adult correctional institutions or the state reformatory for women." In any case, we must begin by finding their victims, in the hope that this will lead us to the murderers who, as defined by law, are guilty of the crimes. That search will be frustrating.

Suppose that a corpse is found by the police or by someone who notifies them. Was the death due to natural causes, accident, suicide, or criminal homicide? In some cases no one will be able to answer this question categorically, and thus a successful murder may remain hidden. Some deaths may never become known. The number of missing persons reported annually to the authorities is large and among those never located some may have been murdered and their bodies disposed of without trace. If the police or medical examiners do conclude that a death was due to foul play, would they be able to give it the legal label of murder, specifically capital murder? It is conceivable that this could be done with reasonable certainty in the case of gangland killings, which bear the stamp of a characteristic technique, and in felony-murders, where the objective circumstances of the crimes determine their classification as first-degree murders. But the classification of many, perhaps most, homicides as capital murder is simply impossible until the killer is arrested, the circumstances of the crime clarified, and intent and premeditation conclusively established.

If this is a correct description of the process of discovery, we cannot expect to find the victims of capital murder subclassified as such among the "deaths due to homicide" recorded by medical examiners, nor among the "murders" or "murders and nonnegligent manslaughters" known to police agencies.[10] Neither could the police completely segregate

---

10. Nearly half a century ago I concluded that the number of certain serious crimes, among them criminal homicide, known to the police should be used for the construction of crime rates, because "due to a number of variable elements represented by changes in administrative policies and efficiency *the value of a crime rate for index purposes decreases as the distance from the crime itself, in terms of procedure, increases.* In other words, police statistics, particularly those of 'crimes known to the police,' are most likely to furnish a good basis for a crime index" (Thorsten Sellin, "The Basis of a Crime Index," *Journal of Criminal Law and Criminology,*

capital murderers from other killers in the statistics of suspects arrested for willful homicide. We are led inexorably to the conclusion that the information we need to determine the success or failure of retribution can be found mainly in records and statistics of the administration of criminal justice, since courts decide which defendants should be labeled capital murderers. The total number of such adjudicated offenders will only be a sample, albeit a fairly large one, since among crimes against the person homicides have very high reporting and "clearance" rates, but nevertheless, only a sample of the total number of capital murderers, which is unknowable. This poses a serious problem for researchers who need to construct murder and especially capital murder rates.

It is unfortunate that we have to depend on judicial data for answers, because among the statistical series of data about crime and criminals in the United States, our judicial statistics are the poorest.[11] Even in the few states that have respectable bureaus of criminal statistics which issue annual reports on the administration of justice, it is rare to find data on *capital* murders or murderers. They are usually concealed within the data on murderers in general or even within the broader category of willful homicides, which includes voluntary manslaughter. There is, of course, a good argument for ignoring the distinction between first-degree murders punishable by death and murders in the second degree not so punishable, because the line drawn between them is tenuous and it is only too common to find a capital murder reduced to

---

vol. 22, 1931, p. 346). This conclusion has been generally accepted by statisticians and criminologists in the United States and abroad, but it should be noted that I was not referring to murder, still less to capital murder, but to the more inclusive class of criminal homicide.

11. In Chapter 4 of his *History and Organization of Criminal Statistics in the United States* (Boston: Houghton-Mifflin & Co., 1911), Louis N. Robinson noted that of 25 states which published some sort of judicial statistics, only Ohio was given a "good" mark. The statistics of Maine, Indiana, Michigan, and Iowa were rated "fairly good" and those of Alabama as "well summarized and seemingly complete," but the statistics of the rest of the states he judged to be useless.

a lower degree by prosecutors who find it expedient to do so in order to ensure a conviction, or by juries reluctant to expose a defendant to a death sentence and possible execution. Yet, if we want a clearer picture of how the "law of talion" operates, we need to separate capital murderers from the rest. Statistics permitting this separation are not easy to find.

In order to arrive — after some digression — at a tentative determination of the number of known capital murderers, we shall (1) first look at the number and percentage of murderers among those involved in willful homicides and (2) the number and percentage of capital murderers among murderers. Since the execution of a murderer is the goal of the law of talion, (3) the risk of execution will be examined and, since this law, in principle, requires that it be applied evenhandedly, we shall (4) look for some evidence of that fact.

Proportion of Murderers Among Willful Homicides

In 1932, the federal Bureau of the Census initiated a program designed to secure statistical data concerning the administration of criminal justice by courts of general trial jurisdiction in the states of the union. Excluding the first experimental year, the number of jurisdictions from which data were gathered during 1933-1945 varied between twenty-four and thirty annually. Sixteen states[12] and the District of Columbia reported regularly. All but one — New Mexico — were in the North, and all but three — Minnesota, Rhode Island, and Wisconsin — were death penalty jurisdictions. Other states reported less frequently.[13] Altogether, the number of

---

12. Idado, Iowa, Kansas, Minnesota, Montana, New Hampshire, New Jersey, New Mexico, Ohio, Oregon, Pennsylvania, Rhode Island, South Dakota, Utah, Washington, and Wisconsin.
13. Colorado, Connecticut, and North Dakota: 12 years; Massachusetts: 11; Vermont: 10; New York: 9; Michigan: 8; Arizona and Indiana: 5; Nebraska: 3; Illinois and Maine: 2; and Delaware, Missouri, and Texas: 1. Of these, Maine, North Dakota, and Michigan were abolitionist states.

annual reports reached 341, including 60 from abolitionist states. Among the data reported were the number of defendants prosecuted, convicted, and sentenced for murder and manslaughter. They are consolidated in Table 2.1.

Table 2.1: Willful Homicides, 1933-1945

States	Defendants	Prosecuted for			
		Murder	%	Manslaughter	%
With Death Penalty	27,640	11,838	42.8	15,802	57.2
Abolitionist	2,780	949	34.1	1,831	65.9
Total	30,420	12,787	42.0	17,633	58.0
		Convicted of			
With Death Penalty	15,184	6,670	43.9	8,514	56.1
Abolitionist	1,722	606	35.2	1.116	64.8
Total	16,906	7,276	43.0	9,630	57.0

SOURCE: *Judicial Criminal Statistics* (Washington, DC: Bureau of the Census)

Of course, the number of defendants in homicide cases does not equal the number of victims, which is the number counted in all police reports of known offenses. Some defendants killed more than one person and two or more were at times involved in the killing of a single person. Nevertheless, it is safe to infer from the data presented in the table that fewer than half of the defendants prosecuted or convicted of willful homicides were murderers as defined by law, and that the proportions were smaller in abolition states than in death

penalty states. The percentage was 42.8 for defendants prosecuted and 43.9 for defendants convicted in death penalty
states; corresponding figures for abolitionist states were 34.1
percent and 35.2 percent. When both of these groups are
merged, the percentages of defendants prosecuted and convicted for murder were nearly identical — 42 and 43.

These percentages hide considerable differences among the
jurisdictions, however. In Table 2.2 only those providing a
death penalty for murder and reporting to the Bureau of the
Census for at least nine years are listed. In prosecutions for
willful homicide, New Mexico charged 69.4 percent of the
defendants with murder, while Connecticut charged only 20.7
percent. In New Mexico, 68.9 percent of those convicted were
found guilty of murder; in Connecticut, 23 percent. The rest of
the jurisdictions showed ratios somewhere between these ex-
tremes.

When we examine the judicial statistics of individual states,
the percentages of murderers in prosecutions or convictions
of willful homicides may also be seen to vary from year to
year. To illustrate this fact Tables 2.3 and 2.4 present data
from Massachusetts and California for relatively recent
periods. In California's prosecutions for wilful homicide, the
percentage of murderers is nearly double that of
Massachusetts and in convictions about one-third greater. Incidentally, the statistical reports of Massachusetts on which
Table 2.3 is based permit a check on the accuracy of the data
reported by that state to the Bureau of the Census during
1936-1945. The data on convictions appear to be quite
reliable. The reasons for the discrepancies in the data on prosecutions are not clear.

One inference that can be drawn from an inspection of the
foregoing tables is that the Federal Bureau of Investigation's
assertion that 18,780 "murders" were committed in the
United States in 1976 is indefensible to say the least.[14] This

---

14. *Crime in the United States, 1976. Uniform Crime Reports* (Washington, DC:
Department of Justice, 1977), p. 7.

Table 2.2: Percentage of Murderers Among Those Prosecuted or Convicted of Willful Homicide: Death Penalty States, 1933-1945

	Defendants Prosecuted			Defendants Convicted		
State	Total	Murder	%	Total	Murder	%
California[a]	3,028	1,368	45.2	1,836	827	45.0
Colorado	849	529	62.3	425	256	60.2
Connecticut[b]	576	119	20.7	408	94	23.0
District of Columbia	767	410	53.5	408	188	46.1
Idaho	226	104	46.0	139	60	43.2
Iowa	464	229	49.4	288	152	52.8
Kansas	736	475	64.5	450	287	63.8
Massachusetts[c]	597	191	32.0	341	107	31.3
Montana	218	123	56.4	120	71	59.2
New Hampshire	90	28	31.0	57	20	35.1
New Jersey	2,007	801	39.9	916	470	51.3
New Mexico	742	515	69.4	387	253	68.9
New York[d]	2,690	1,007	37.4	1,818	621	34.2
Ohio	3,641	1,592	43.7	2,289	823	36.0
Oregon	322	126	39.1	186	79	42.5
Pennsylvania	7,063	2,253	31.9	3,172	1,300	41.0
South Dakota	111	40	36.0	65	23	35.4
Utah	231	89	38.5	134	52	38.8
Vermont[e]	49	28	57.1	18	8	44.4
Washington	819	288	35.2	546	192	35.2
Wyoming	147	94	63.9	86	53	61.6
Total	25,373	10,409	41.0	14,089	5,936	42.1

SOURCE: *Judicial Criminal Statistics* (Washington, DC: Bureau of the Census).

a. Participated 1934-1938, 1940-1945.
b. 1934-1945.
c. 1935-1945.
d. 1937-1945.
e. 1933, 1935-1943.

Table 2.3: Willful Homicide: Massachusetts, 1931-1970

Quinquennia	Defendants Prosecuted			Defendants Convicted		
	Total	Murder	%	Total	Murder	%
1966-1970	900	444	49.4	421	147	34.9
1961-1965	638	290	45.5	309	100	32.4
1956-1960	453	193	42.6	223	70	31.4
1951-1955	362	155	42.8	165	48	29.1
1946-1950	413	204	49.4	193	87	45.3
1941-1945	463	195	42.1	162	43	26.5
1936-1940	528	215	40.7	127	53	41.7
1931-1935	676	254	37.6	195	60	30.8
1931-1970	4,433	1,950	44.0	1,794	608	33.9

NOTE: Compiled from data in Commonwealth of Massachusetts, *Annual Report* (after 1940, *Statistical Reports*) *of the Commissioner of Correction,* Boston (Public Document No. 115).

Table 2.4: Willful Homicide: California, 1952-1966

Quinquennia	Defendants Prosecuted			Defendants Convicted		
	Total	Murder	%	Total	Murder	%
1962-1966	2,934	2,511	85.6	2.046	982	48.0
1957-1961	1,967	1,727	87.8	1,477	765	51.8
1952-1956	1,458	1,099	75.4	990	521	52.6
1952-1966	6,359	5,337	83.9	4,513	2,268	50.3

NOTE: Compiled from data in Bureau of Criminal Statistics, *Crime in California* (after 1964, *Crime and Delinquency in California*), Annual Reports, Sacramento. After 1966, only willful homicides, including murder and voluntary manslaughter, are given in the reports.

Table 2.5: Percentage of Defendants in Willful Homicide Cases Prosecuted or Convicted for Murder: Massachusetts, 1936-1945

During	Defendants Prosecuted			Defendants Convicted		
	Total	Murder	%	Total	Murder	%
1936-1940						
(a)	228	86	37.7	127	53	41.7
(b)	528	215	40.7	127	53	41.7
1941-1945						
(a)	236	70	29.7	159	41	25.8
(b)	463	195	42.1	162	43	26.5

SOURCES: (a) Bureau of the Census, *Judicial Criminal Statistics;*
(b) Annual Reports of the Commissioner of Correction.

figure is, in fact, the estimated number of all willful homicides known to the police that year. Murder, as defined by law, is certainly willful homicide, but the Bureau knows well that all such crimes are not murder. If we can assume that the proportion of murder victims is about the same as the proportion of murderers among adjudicated defendants in cases of willful homicide, there were probably fewer than 9000 known murders in 1976.

Proportion of Capital Murderers Among Murderers

We noted earlier that it is often difficult to separate capital from noncapital murder, because these labels, attached to the crimes by grand juries, prosecutors, or trial juries, may be arbitrarily chosen by the labelers to expedite justice or justify the verdict in a given case. Hence, one might argue that those indicted or prosecuted for murder should be the group whose ultimate fate would illustrate the operation of the law of talion. On the other hand, we know that legislatures have reserved the death penalty for only some murderers. Therefore, logic demands that we should attempt to sort out the number of capital murderers processed and finally disposed of by courts. Official statistical series enabling one to engage in such an exercise are scarce. The few, random illustrations that follow are simply offered to show the strange dimensions of the problem.

From the judicial statistics found in the annual reports of the Secretary of State of Ohio, the number of those prosecuted for capital murder can be extracted from the number of prosecutions for murder in that state. A compilation of data from these reports for the years 1881-1904 is summarized in Table 2.6. Except for the earliest five-year period, the rest show that about half of those charged with murder were accused of a capital crime. The percentage for the nineteen years covered by the table was 52.8. The selected years after 1904 show variations, but taken togegether, those charged with capital murder constituted 49.6 percent of the prosecutions for murder.

Table 2.6: Defendants Prosecuted for Murder: Ohio, 1886-1904

Years[a]	Total	Capital Murder	%	Year[b]	Total	Capital Murder	%
1901-1904	347	172	49.6	1930	176	87	49.4
1896-1900	271	136	50.2	1920	132	81	61.4
1891-1895	312	161	51.6	1911	94	40	42.5
1886-1890	318	190	59.7	1907	88	35	39.8
Total	1,248	659	52.8	Total	490	243	49.6

a. Ohio State Library, *Monthly Bulletin* 1, no. 10, January 1906, p. 9.
b. Secretary of State, *Annual Report,* Columbus.

Table 2.7: Defendants in Murder Cases:
Massachusetts, 1931-1970

Years	Defendants Prosecuted	Defendants Convicted	%	Sentenced for Capital Murder[a]	% of Prosecuted	% of Convicted
1966-1970	444	147	33.1	55	12.4	37.4
1961-1965	290	100	34.5	31	10.7	31.0
1956-1960	193	70	36.3	9	4.7	12.8
1951-1955	155	48	31.0	9	5.8	18.6
1946-1950	204	87	42.6	14	6.8	16.1
1941-1945	195	43	22.1	8	4.1	18.6
1936-1940	215	53	24.6	9	4.2	17.0
1931-1935	254	60	23.6	17	6.7	28.3
Total	1,950	608	31.1	152	7.8	25.0

SOURCE: See Table 2.3.

a. The number of those committed to state prisons or reformatories, including those to be executed.

Table 2.7 reveals that the conviction ratios of those prosecuted for murder in Massachusetts during the forty years,
1931-1970, ranged from 22.1 to 42.6 percent, and prison
commitments for capital murder (including those committed
for execution) from 4.1 to 12.4 percent. In Table 2.8, recent
data from Pennsylvania indicate that during 1971-1975 the
percentages of defendants in murder cases who were charged
with first-degree murder varied from 5.5 to 39.7, the last two
years showing the higher percentages. It may be that the rein-
troduction of the death penalty in March 1974 was to some
degree responsible for the rise which is also noticeable in the
proportion of convictions for capital murder, which was only
2.8 percent of the prosecutions in 1971 but 14.8 and 20.2 per-

cent in the last two years. During the three biennia examined, the proportions of murder defendants in Alabama charged with capital murder varied from 51 to 70 percent, and the convictions for that crime from 25 to 34.2 percent.

Table 2.8: Defendants in Murder Cases: Pennsylvania, 1971-1975

Years	Total Prosecuted	Capital Murder	%	Convicted of Capital Murder	% of Prosecuted	% of Convicted
1975	688	273	39.7	139	20.2	50.9
1974	627	133	21.2	93	14.8	70.0
1973	648	41	6.3	26	4.0	63.4
1972	508	66	13.0	34	6.7	51.5
1971	866	48	5.5	24	2.8	50.0
Total	3,337	561	16.8	316	9.5	56.3

SOURCE: Bureau of Criminal Justice Statistics, *Pennsylvania Criminal Court Dispositions,* Department of Justice, Harrisburg (annual report).

Table 2.9: Defendants in Murder Cases: Alabama

Years	Defendants Prosecuted	Defendants Convicted	%	Sentenced for Capital Murder[a]	% of Prosecuted	% of Convicted
1924-1926	432	293	67.8	108	25.0	36.8
1920-1922	465	326	70.1	159	34.2	48.7
1908-1910	468	239	51.1	124	26.5	51.9
Total	1,365	858	62.8	391	28.6	45.6

SOURCE: *Biennial Report of the Attorney General of Alabama,* Montgomery.

Of a total of 4982 adults committed to the prisons of
California in 1950-1975 with sentences for murder, 2111 (42.2
percent) had been convicted of capital murder. Only 8 percent (437) of the murder convicts and 20.7 percent (104) of
those convicted of capital murder were sentenced to die.[15]

This admittedly superficial examination of judicial
statistics was stimulated by a wish to discover if the
retributive aim of the death penalty is achieved. As such, it
serves only to furnish a few preliminary data of the kind
needed to seek an answer to the question: Do murderers
receive the punishment they deserve — death — as advocated
by supporters of the law of talion? We have noted that to arrive at a conclusive answer we should establish how many
murderers there are in a death penalty state and then observe
what happens to them. We have noted, however, that the law
threatens only certain murderers with death, because
legislators have fixed different retributive punishments for
the rest. Therefore, we should specifically know how many
capital murderers there are, since they alone are threatened
with extinction. That number is unknowable, however,
because some of them cannot be discovered, and since the
law defines capital murders as acts committed by persons in-
tentionally, premeditatedly, with "malice aforethought" (except when it is through a by-product of a robbery or some
other specified felony), they cannot, in most cases, be so
designated by the police who investigate homicides; nor can
the police, in most cases, accurately label as a capital
murderer a person arrested for homicide. We are, perforce,
compelled to look for him among those prosecuted for
murder. The ultimate determination of who is a capital
murderer is made by the criminal himself, who pleads guilty
to that crime, or by jury or judge after his trial, and if he is
sentenced to death and if he is afterwards executed, the law of

---

15. Based on Table 35 in *California Prisoners 1973* and *California Prisoners 1974
and 1975.* Sacramento: Department of Corrections.

talion has finally been applied.[16]

From the data presented in earlier pages it would appear that roughly half of the defendants in willful homicide cases were charged with murder and about half of these — or about one-fourth of the willful homicide defendants — were prosecuted for capital murder. Local and temporal exceptions to these generalizations are obvious from the tables, but whatever may be the sociocultural, including legal and administrative, factors that influence the categorization and the flow of willful homicide cases through the criminal justice channels, it remains that the factual operation of the law of talion can be observed only in the way defendants in murder cases are disposed of. Whether these defendants constitute a large or a small proportion of the "real" murderers in a population is immaterial. The law of talion can be applied only to murderers who are caught. In the last analysis, its success is measured by the relative number of those sentenced to death and executed. The likelihood that this will be the fate of the murderer will be examined in a later chapter.

---

16. An excellent analysis of the judicial process in capital cases is found in Charles L. Black, Jr.'s *Capital Punishment: The Inevitability of Caprice and Mistake* (New York: W. W. Norton, 1974).

Chapter 3

UNEQUAL JUSTICE

If justice requires that a murderer pay with his life for his crime, neither his social status nor other conditions, which set him apart from his fellowmen, should save him from his fate. All that would be needed would be the determination by a court of justice that the death of a human being was caused by a person, mentally sound and old enough to be held responsible, [under circumstances that made his conduct a capital offense as defined by law.] Equality before the law, which is a foundation stone of democracy, is also a principle basic to the law of talion, but experience tells us that retributive capital justice is tainted by bias and by the influence of factors beyond the control of courts of justice, such as the poverty of the defendant, which prevents him from engaging competent counsel skilled in the art of criminal defense.[1] Of these factors, only two will be briefly examined here, namely, the effect of race bias, specifically bias against blacks, on the administration of justice in murder cases and the chivalrous treatment of female murderers.

---

1. See the chapter on "The Warping Effects of Race and Poverty" in Charles L. Black, Jr.'s book previously cited.

The Role of Race

H. C. Brearley wrote, in 1930, that

a study of the reports of the attorney general of South
Carolina for the years 1920-1926 shows that . . . of the persons
accused of homicide, the whites were found guilty in only
31.7 percent of the cases, while the Negroes were in 64.1 of
the verdicts. . . . This difference is due, doubtless, to such
factors as race prejudice by white jurors and court officials
and the Negro's low economic status, which prevents him
from securing "good" criminal lawyers for his defense. In
South Carolina, consequently, for the years 1915-1927 seven
whites and 53 Negroes suffered capital punishment, one white
for every 101 white homicides and one Negro for every 38
Negro homicides.[2]

The conviction differentials noted by Brearley are verifiable
by a look at Table 3.1, also based on the annual reports of the
Attorney General of South Carolina, but limited to murder
cases. When charged with murder, black males stood a
chance of conviction about double that for white males. That
chance was even greater when black and white females are
compared. Incidentally, while nine out of ten black females
were convicted of manslaughter, no white woman was prosecuted for that crime during the three years covered.

Because the biennial reports of the Attorney General of
Arkansas used to print lists of those prosecuted in the judicial
districts as reported by the prosecuting attorneys, giving the
name, color, sex, crime charged, and disposition of each
defendant, the effect of race on dispositions in that state can
be ascertained. During the eight years, 1912-1916 and
1921-1924, indictments were returned either for murder,
without designating the degree, or for murder in the first or
the second degree. The following tables illustrate how murder

2. "The Negro and Homicide," *Social Forces,* vol. 9, 1930, p. 252.

Table 3.1: Murder Prosecutions: South Carolina

Sex	Year	Black			White		
		No.	Gulty	%	No.	Guilty	%
Males	1938	119	82	68.9	77	27	35.1
	1927	98	57	58.2	60	20	33.3
	1923	102	63	61.8	90	20	22.2
	Total	319	202	63.3	227	67	29.5
Females	1938	21	16	76.2	3	1	33.3
	1927	15	10	66.6	4	2	50.0
	1923	17	12	70.6	4	—	0.0
	Total	53	38	71.7	11	3	27.2

SOURCE: *Annual Reports of the Attorney General of South Carolina.*

defendants in general were disposed of and how defendants specifically charged with capital murder were treated. Table 3.2 shows, for instance, that the percentage of blacks charged with and convicted of murder was much higher than that of whites — 71.6 versus 53.2 — and that of white males, one out of six was convicted of the lesser offense of manslaughter, compared to one of nine blacks. Only 10 percent of black males and 15 percent of black females were acquitted; the corresponding figures for whites were 25 percent and 55 percent.

Women were rarely charged with capital murder. Of four blacks so charged in 1923-1924, one was found guilty but sentenced to only one year's imprisonment; two were convicted of manslaughter and given sentences of one and two years. The two white women were convicted of second-degree murder and sentenced to fifteen years and life, respectively. Table 3.3, therefore, deals only with males. Here, too, whites were favored. Although the percentages of blacks and whites

Table 3.2: Defendants Disposed of in Murder Cases, All Degrees: Arkansas, 1912-1916, 1921-1924

| | Males | | | | Females | | | |
| | Blacks | | Whites | | Blacks | | Whites | |
Disposition	No.	%	No.	%	No.	%	No.	%
Guilty	492	71.6	375	53.2	50	54.3	11	35.5
Acquitted	70	10.2	177	25.1	14	15.2	17	54.8
Guilty of Manslaughter	53	7.7	63	8.9	12	13.1	—	—
Dismissed or Nolle Prossed	72	10.5	90	12.8	16	17.4	3	9.6
Total	687	100.0	705	100.0	92	100.0	31	99.9

SOURCE: *Biennial Reports of the Attorney General of Arkansas.*

found guilty of capital murder were nearly the same, 71.2 percent of the blacks and 55.6 percent of the whites were convicted of some degree of criminal homicide, and 25 percent of the blacks and 17 percent of the whites guilty of capital murder received sentences of death. Two of the four blacks so sentenced were executed, but only one of the six whites. Equally interesting is the distribution of sentences given to those convicted. We have already noted the disposition of women in capital cases. Now, of eight white women prosecuted for murder in 1923-1924, one was convicted and sentenced to imprisonment for four years. Of eleven black women, one was sentenced to two years, one to three years, four to five years, one to thirteen years, one to twenty-one years, and one to life imprisonment. No white woman was prosecuted for second-degree murder, and the case of the only black woman charged with that crime was nolle prossed. The sentences imposed on male defendants are found in Tables 3.4 to 3.6, separately covering defendants charged

Table 3.3: Male Defendants Disposed of in Capital Murder Cases: Arkansas, 1923-1924

Disposition	Black No.	Black %	White No.	White %
Guilty	16	30.8	35	33.0
Convicted of Murder Second Degree	14	26.9	16	15.1
Convicted of Manslaughter	7	13.5	8	7.5
Acquitted	3	5.7	14	13.2
Dismissed or Nolle Prossed	8	15.4	27	25.5
Sentenced to Death	4	7.7	6	5.7
Total	52	100.0	106	100.0
Executed	2		1	

SOURCE: See Table 3.2.

with murder, and second-degree murder, and capital murder.

The ratio of whites found guilty of murder as charged was, in fact, slightly higher than that for blacks, but blacks so charged were convicted of second-degree murder in 21.4 percent of the cases, compared with 9.3 percent for whites, who were more likely to be convicted of the lesser crime of manslaughter — 16.7 percent of the whites and 8.3 percentof the blacks. One black was sentenced to death but not executed, which suggests that some of the general murder indictments actually included cases of capital murder.

Few males were originally charged with second-degree murder, four blacks and eighteen whites. Three of the blacks were sentenced for the crime, two to five and one to fifteen years; one was convicted of involuntary manslaughter and sent to prison for a year. Of the fourteen whites for whom sentences were recorded, half were sentenced for manslaughter.

Table 3.4: Sentences of Male Defendants Charged with Murder: Arkansas, 1923-1924

Sentenced to	Blacks (84)			Whites (54)			
	Murder	Murder 2	Involuntary Manslaughter	Murder	Murder 2	Voluntary Manslaughter	Involuntary Manslaughter
60 days			1				1
3 months							
6 months							
1 year	3	1	1	2		1	1
2 years	6		2	3	1	1	
3 years	1		1	1		3	
4 years			2			2	
5 years	7	9		9	1		
6 years				1			
7 years	10			2	2		
9 years	1						
10 years	2			4			
12 years	5	1		1	1[a]		
15 years	2			1			
18 years	1						
21 years	5	7		6			
Life	15			9			
Death	1						
Not given				1			
Total	59	18	7	40	5	7	2

SOURCE: See Table 3.2.

a. Sentence suspended.

Table 3.5: Sentences of Male Defendants in Second-Degree Murder Cases: Arkansas, 1923-1924

Sentenced to	Blacks (4)			Whites (18)		
	Murder 2	Manslaughter	Involuntary Manslaughter	Murder 2	Manslaughter	Involuntary Manslaughter
1 year			1	1	1	1
2 years						2
3 years					1	
5 years	2			4	2	
7 years				1		
15 years	1			1		
21 years				1		
Not given				4		
Total	3		1	11	4	3

SOURCE: See Table 3.2.

Table 3.6: Sentences of Male Defendants in Capital Murder Cases: Arkansas, 1923-1924

Sentenced to	Blacks (37)			Whites (59)		
	Capital Murder	Murder 2	Manslaughter	Capital Murder	Murder 2	Manslaughter
1 year				1		
2 years			4	2	1	6
3 years						2
5 years		4		2	8	
7 years		3		3	1	
8 years					1	
10 years		3			1	
12 years		1				
14 years					1	
15 years	1					
21 years	2	2			2	
Life	8			18		
Death	4			6		
Not given	1	1	3	3	1	
Total	16	14	7	35	16	8
Executed	2			1		

SOURCE: See Table 3.2.

Table 3.6 tells us what happened to the defendants indicted for first-degree murder, placing their lives at stake. The ratios of sentences for both degrees of murder combined were about equal for blacks and whites — 87.5 and 85.5 percent — but a larger proportion of whites, 68.6 percent, than of blacks, 53.3 percent, were sentenced for capital murder; this would appear to favor blacks. An examination of the sentences shows, however, that no black received a sentence shorter than fifteen years and that four of sixteen were sentenced to death, of whom two were executed. Of the thirty-two whites with known sentences, 25 percent received prison sentences of from one to seven years. The proportion of life sentences was the same for both races, but of six whites sentenced to death, only one was executed.

Some would argue that the racial inequalities noted in the disposition of murder cases do not reflect racial prejudice but actual differences in the quality of murders committed by blacks and whites. No such qualitative differences have been established, however, but what can be demonstrated is that in states where racial attitudes rooted in what was once a slave-owning society still persist, "unequal justice" flourishes when the victims of blacks are not other blacks but whites. This aspect of the administration of capital justice in murder cases has received little attention from researchers. There exist persuasive studies of the effect of the race of the offender on the disposition of his case and his punishment, when he is charged with rape and his victim is, or is not, of the same race,[3] but similar investigations of homicide are extremely

---

3. Statement of Professor Marvin E. Wolfgang before Subcommittee No. 3 of the Committee on the Judiciary of the United States House of Representatives on proposed legislation for a moratorium on capital punishment (Hart-Celler Hearings, March 16, 1972, pp. 174-180, 182, 183). Published as "Racial Discrimination in the Death Sentence for Rape," in William J. Bowers, *Executions in America* (Lexington, MA: D. C. Heath, 1974), pp. 109-120. See also Marvin E. Wolfgang and Marc Riedel, "Rape, Racial Discrimination and the Death Penalty," in Hugo Adam Bedau, ed., *Capital Punishment in the United States* (New York: AMS Press, 1975), pp. 99-121.

rare. A study[4] of cases in ten North Carolina counties for the
period 1930-1940 arrived at the results shown in Table 3.7.
When the defendant was black and his victim white, he was
sentenced to death in 43 percent of the cases; but if the defen-
dent was white and his victim black, he ran no such risk at all.
When blacks murdered blacks, only 5 percent of them received death sentences; 15 percent of whites murdering whites
were sentenced to death. Unfortunately, there was no follow-
up showing whether nor not these sentences were executed.
This did interest the author of an earlier study[5] who examined
homicides in North Carolina during 1933-1939 (Table 3.8). In
intraracial murders, the ratios of death sentences commuted
were about the same for blacks and whites, but when the offender was black and his victim white, his chance of receiving
a commutation was one in five, instead of one in three. For
the first time since Reconstruction days, a white man was executed for murdering a black. He was a disreputable low-
class fellow whose victim was an old and highly respected
Negro in his community. We have already noted that in the
beinnium 1923-1924 in Arkansas two of four blacks sentenced to die for murder were executed, but only one of six
whites. During 1914-1958, those convited of capital murder
and placed on death row in Pennsylvania numbered 439. Of
147 blacks, 11.6 percent received commutations; while of 263
whites, 20.3 percent were granted that boon.[6] Of 37 whites
and 23 blacks received in Ohio prisons during 1950-1959 with
death sentences or already serving sentences commuted to
life, 49 percent of the whites but only 22 percent of the blacks
benefited from such commutations. Incicentally, the "warp-

4. Harold Garfinkel, "Inter- and Intra-racial Homicides," in Marvin E. Wolfgang,
ed., *Studies in Homicide* (New York: Harper & Row, 1967), pp. 46-65.
5. Guy B. Johnson, "The Negro and Crime," *Annals of the American Academy of
Political and Social Science,* vol. 217, 1941, p. 100.
6. Marvin E. Wolfgang, Arlene Kelly, and Hans C. Nolde, "Comparisons of the
Executed and Commuted among Admissions to Death Row," *Journal of Criminal
Law, Criminology and Police Science,* vol. 53, 1962, p. 306.

ing effects of poverty'' may be seen in the fact that of those who had been represented by court-appointed counsel, only 30.6 percent received commutations, compared with 44.4 percent of those having private counsel.[7]

Table 3.7: Race of Defendants and Victims in Capital Murder Cases: North Carolina, 1930-1940

Disposition	Black/White	White/Black	Black/Black	White/White
Acquitted	6	3	65	28
Convicted and Sentenced to	35	8	307	73
Less than life	16	8	291	59
Life	4	—	1	3
Death	15	—	15	11

NOTE: Ten counties (Alamance, Caswell, Chatham, Durham, Granville, Guilford, Orange, Person, Rockingham and Wake).

Table 3.8: Death Sentences and Executions for Murder: North Carolina, 1933-1939

Race of Murderer and Victim	Death Sentence	Commuted	Executed No.	Executed %
Black/White	36	7	29	80.5
White/Black	1	—	1	—
Black/Black	45	16	29	64.4
White/White	41	13	28	68.3

SOURCE: Johnson, op. cit., Table 2.

---

7. Ohio Legislative Service Commission, *Capital Punishment,* Columbus, January 1961 (Staff Research Report No. 46), pp. 62-63.

The Role of Sex

"There can be little doubt," wrote Raymond Bye, "That the death penalty is in fact a dead letter so far as women are concerned, because juries simply refuse to send members of the weaker sex to their death."[8] This statement is not completely accurate but contains a kernel of truth. Women do commit fewer murders than do men, partly because they rarely engage in the commission of felonies that might end in charges of felony-murder, and partly because, on the whole, they live more sheltered lives. Even so, the fact that in 38 years, 1930-1967, only 30 (.8 percent) of the 3334 persons executed for murder in the United States were women suggests that Bye's statement is not too far from the mark, and that the law of talion is not applied to women murderers as often as it is to men. Some evidence has already been presented in earlier pages. In Ohio, during 1955-1958, there were 286 men and 50 women prosecuted for first-degree murder. Of the men, 89 (31 percent) were found guilty as charged, but only four (8 percent) of the women. No women, but 8 percent of the men, were sentenced to death.[9]

The rarity of executions of women is seen from Table 3.9. Of more than 40 death penalty states, only 17 reported such executions during the periods indicated. The end of the period for each state is the year of the last execution regardless of sex. All executions stopped after 1967 by order of the Supreme Court of the United States. Of the 35 women executed, 7 of the 33 whose race is known were black — one each in Alabama, Georgia, New York, North Carolina, Ohio, South Carolina, and Virginia. The California cases illustrate the stringent selection by the courts when women murderers are sentenced. In contrast, of the 1022 males con-

---

8. Raymond T. Bye, *Capital Punishment in the United States* (Philadelphia: Committee on Philanthropic Labor of Philandelphia, Yearly Meeting of Friends, 1918), p. 49.
9. Ohio Legislative Service Commission, *op. cit.*, p. 61.

Table 3.9: Proportion of Women Among Murderers Executed

State	Period	Women Executed	All Executions	Percentage Women	Last Woman Executed
Alabama	1927-1965	3	131	2.3	1957
Arizona	1910-1916 1918-1963	1	63	1.6	1930
California	1893-1967	4	494	.8	1962
Delaware	1830-1946	1	8	12.5	1935
Georgia	1924-1964	1	349	.3	1945
Illinois	1928-1962	1	97	1.0	1938
Louisiana	1930-1961	2	116	1.1	1942
Mississippi	1930-1964	1	130	.7	1937
Missouri	1930-1965	1	31	3.2	1953
New York	1890-1963	8	691	1.2	1951
North Carolina	1910-1961	2	282	.7	1944
Ohio	1885-1963	3	343	.9	1954
Pennsylvania	1915-1962	2	350	.6	1946
South Carolina	1912-1962	2	182	1.1	1947
Vermont	1864-1954	2	21	9.5	1905
Virginia	1903-1962	1	176	.5	1912
Total		35	3,464	1.0	

SOURCES: William J. Bowers, *Executions in America* (Lexington, Mass.: D. C. Heath, 1974); N. P. S. Bulletin, no. 42, June 1968; *Executions, 1930-1967* (Washington, DC: U.S. Department of Justice, Bureau of Prisons).

victed of capital murder in that state during 1950-1967, only 295 (28.8 percent) were sentenced to death and of these 102 (34.6 percent) were executed. Of the 44 women convicted of capital murder, only 2 were sentenced to die (4.5 percent), and both were executed, one in 1955 and the other in 1962. Previously only two women had been executed in the state. Juanita Spinelli, who went to the gas chamber in 1941, was

the first woman to be legally executed in California. She was
a crafty leader of a "mob" and was executed with two male
accomplices for the murder of a young male subordinate. The
second was Louise Peete, who had been sentenced in 1921 to
life imprisonment for the murder of a mining executive. She
had been paroled in 1939 and in 1944 was convicted again of
capital murder for which she was executed in 1946.[10]

The death penalty has apparently not only failed as an
agent of retribution; its selective application has also grossly
distorted justice.

---

10. Clifton Duffy, with Al Hirschberg, *88 Men and 2 Women* (Garden City, NY:
Doubleday, 1962), pp. 131-134.

Chapter 4

THE RISK FACTOR

What risk of execution does a murder defendant run? If he is prosecuted he runs the risk of conviction, if he is convicted of capital murder he risks being sentenced to death, and if he is so sentenced he risks execution. With each step in this process the risk looms larger. Thus, in the death penalty states reporting to the Bureau of the Census (see Table 2.2), 433 death sentences were imposed on 6.4 percent of those prosecuted for murder. During the reporting period there were 378 executions for murder in these states, i.e., 3.6 percent of the prosecutions, but 80.7 percent of those sentences to death.[1] No attempt to pursue this problem in depth will be made here; only a few illustrations showing the dimensions of the risk factors, past and present, will be given.

---

1. The number of executions has been derived from the state lists of cases reproduced in William J. Bowers, *Executions in America* (Lexington, MA: D. C. Heath, 1974). They have one inevitable defect. Those executed during a given year include few sentenced to death that year. Years may pass before the prisoner is executed. Therefore, the number of executions during a given year in a state is not closely related to the death sentences passed that year, but by consolidating data for a long series of years the relationship between death sentences and executions can be established with reasonable accuracy. Of 238 executions recorded during 1870-1911 from 51 of the 56 judicial districts in Pennsylvania, 70 occurred the same year as the sentence, 152 the next year, 15 the year following, and 1 three years from the year of the sentence. See Robert Ralston, *The Delay in the Execution of Murderers* (Pennsylvania Bar Association, 1911). In recent decades these delays have increased in length.

During 1931-1950, a murder defendant in Massachusetts faced a 29 percent risk of being convicted and 4.2 risk of being sentenced to death. If he was convicted that risk rose to 14.4 percent, and if he was convicted of capital murder, for which death was the mandatory punishment until 1952, his chance of escaping that fate was 1 in 4; if he was sentenced to die, he still had 1 chance in 4 of cheating the executioner. The decades of 1951-1970 presented a different picture. Of those prosecuted for murder, 33.7 percent were convicted and 6.6 percent sentenced to death but risked no execution. No one had been put to death since May, 1947.[2] A special study of first-degree murder convictions, 1900-1962, showed that during this century until May 9, 1947, 87 men and 1 woman had been sentenced to death in Massachusetts. The woman's sentence was commuted, and 75 percent of the men were executed. During the subsequent period, of 30 men convicted none was executed.[3]

During 1881-1904, the chance of a person prosecuted for murder in Ohio being convicted was 52.8 percent and of being sentenced to death about 1 in 20. If he was convicted, he received a death sentence in one out of ten cases, and ran a 68.5 percent risk of being executed.[4] In Georgia, during 1926-1935, death sentences were imposed on 2.6 percent of defendants in murder cases, on 4.8 percent of those convicted, and on 9.8 percent of those convicted of capital murder. Eight out of ten of these were executed.[5]

In Pennsylvania, 1971-1975, only three persons were received in state prisons with sentences to death (but were not

---

2. See Table 2.3 for source.
3. William F. Bugden, *An Analysis of Convictions of Murder in the First Degree in Massachusetts from January 1, 1900 to December 31, 1962* (Boston: Department of Correction, n.d.), publication no. 312.
4. See Table 2.6 for source.
5. *Survey of Criminal Court Procedure in Georgia* (Atlanta: State Department of Public Welfare, 1937), based on 57 counties containing over half of the state's population.

executed), although 3337 were prosecuted, 1851 (55.5 percent) convicted of murder, and 266 of these (14.3 percent) convicted of capital murder; 47.4 percent of those prosecuted for capital murder were convicted.[6] In Philadelphia, 1925-1934, death sentences were imposed on 2.6 percent of defendants charged with and 6.6 percent of those convicted of murder. Of those sentenced for capital murder (18 percent), about 1 in 5 (18.1 percent) was sentenced to die.[7] During 1961-1968 in Chicago, 18 persons, or .7 percent of 2333 persons charged with and 1.5 percent of 1206 convicted of murder received death sentences.[8]

Of 155 defendants in murder cases in Connecticut in 1907-1930, 43 (60.6 percent) were charged with capital murder, a death sentence being mandatory on conviction. There were 41 executions during the period.[9] In California, 1952-1966, 43 percent of 5287 defendants charged with murder were convicted. There were 90 executions, i.e., 1.7 percent of those charged and 3.9 percent of those convicted of murder were executed.[10] Of 225 persons convicted of capital murder during 1963-1965, one was executed.[11]

Of 7053 adult males committed to California prisons in 1950-1975 after being convicted of felonious homicide, 4632 (65.7 percent) had been convicted of murder, 2026 (28.7 percent) of capital murder, 434 (6.1 percent) had been sentenced

---

6. See Table 2.8 for source; *Capital Punishment,* N.P.S. Bulletin (Washington, DC: U.S. Department of Justice, 1971, 1973, 1975).
7. Sol Black, "Homicides in Philadelphia; a Study of the Procedural Outcome of Defendants Charged with Murder from 1925 to 1934," unpublished seminar paper.
8. Annual reports of the Chicago Crime Commission, prepared by Virgil W. Peterson, Operating Director.
9. Comptroller, Hartford, Connecticut, *Biennial Report of the Criminal Business of the Courts for the Year Ended* , public document no. 27.
10. See Table 2.4 for source.
11. Irwin W. Ramseier, *Willful Homicide in California, 1963-1965* (Sacramento: Bureau of Criminal Statistics, 1967).

to death, and 102 (1.5 percent) were executed. The risk of the death dentence being executed was 23.5 percent.[12]

In Texas, 1946-1967, sentences for murder were given to 4893 defendants. Of these, 139 (2.9 percent) received death sentences. There were 88 executions of murderers — 1.8 percent of all sentences for murder and 63.3 percent of those sentenced to death.[13] In Iowa, 1900-1926, 370 persons were convicted of murder, 167 (45 percent) of capital murder. Of those convicted of murder or capital murder, 9 persons were executed, i.e., 2.4 and 5.4 percent, respectively.

These illustrations show that there was small likelihood that a person prosecuted for murder would be sentenced to death, and that if that occurred no execution would take place in a large proportion of cases, even when the conviction was for capital murder. Considering that these adjudicated murderers were only a part of a group that included the never-discovered offenders and those arrested but not prosecuted or convicted for lack of sufficient evidence, it is obvious that if retribution by death could be measured in relation to the number of *actual* murders, its failure would be even more evident.

In spite of the apparent resurgence of retributive sentiments in recent years and the revival of statutory provisions of capital punishment in most states since the Supreme Court again put its stamp of approval on the death penalty in July 1976, this form of retribution can hardly be said to be meet the expectations of its advocates. Since June 2, 1967, only three persons have been executed in the United States. Yet during 1968-1978, a total of 1697 persons were sentenced to

---

12. Table 35 in *California Prisoners 1973* and *California Prisoners 1974 and 1975* (Sacramento: Department of Corrections).
13. Rupert C. Koeninger, "Capital Punishment in Texas, 1924-1968," *Crime and Delinquency,* vol. 15, 1969, pp. 132-141; Table 1.
14. Data for 1900-1908 from *Report of the Secretary of State Relating to Criminal Convictions* (biennial). Later data from *Report of the Iowa Board of Parole.*

death for murder[15] in states that numbered 7 in 1973 and 23 in 1978. The actual, if not philosophical, repudiation of retribution by death began even before the Supreme Court declared a moratorium on executions in 1967 until it had completed its inquiry into the constitutionality of this punishment. Although the period of 1935-1939 witnessed no fewer than 796 executions for murder in the United States, that number had dropped to 145 in 1960-1964 and to only 7 in 1965, 1 in 1966, and 2 in 1967, even though the 1960s saw a rise in homicide rates. We seem to be torn between a desire to see murderers suffer the ultimate penalty and a reluctance to exact it. Even those who ardently advocate retribution by death often paradocixally stress that it should be used sparingly, for fear that otherwise it would dull our moral sensitivity and lose its terrifying force.

All retributionists would agree that if anybody deserves to die for his crime it is the killer for hire. Many of the present death penalty statutes specifically name this type of murderer, among those deserving execution. Yet the most conspicuous failure of retribution by death is seen in capital murders committed by hired killers and their employers, who are rarely brought to the bar of justice, as all know who have studied organized crime. During 1919-1968, there were 1004 gangland murders in Chicago. Only 17 of them led to the conviction of 23 persons, 4 of whom successfully appealed, 2 of whom were acquitted after trials, and 2 of whom were not tried again. In addition, the case of 1, who was granted a new trial, was nolle prossed. The end result was that of 18 men charged with the murder of 13 persons, 4 were sentenced to life imprisonment and the rest to terms of from 14 to 150 years. *None was sentenced to death.* One of them was actually executed in 1925, but not for the murder which had brought him to prison four years earlier with a sentence of 25

---

15. N.P.S. Bulletin, *Capital Punishment* (Washington, DC: U.S. Department of Justice, annual reports).

years of confinement. He had, with other prisoners, participated in an attempt to escape during which the warden at the Joliet state prison was killed.[16]

---

16. Virgil Peterson, *A Report on Chicago Crime for 1968* (Chicago: Chicago Crime Commission, 1969), pp. 131-132.

Chapter 5

ON GENERAL DETERRENCE

The history of the punishment of criminals is gruesome and was never more so than during the Middle Ages and the early centuries of the modern era. Death was imposed not only for murder but for a number of other crimes against the person and for many offenses against private and public property, rulers, or religion. Executions were cruel and usually designed to prolong the agony of death, as for instance when a criminal was broken "on the wheel" or burned or buried alive. This gave a frightful expression to "the law's demand for retribution, unanimously vindicated by both clerical and worldly authorities on the threshold of the modern age,"[1] which survived, for "even in the eighteenth century, until about 1760, the greater part of Europe regarded the right to punish as founded on the exigencies of public vengeance."[2]

These barbaric punishments were also expected to foster law obedience by the subsidiary deterrent effect they would have on potential offenders, but deeply rooted sentiments of primitive justice, animating the law and its enforcers, called primarily for retribution. Describing the prevailing notions of

1. Joh. Nagler, *Die Strafe* (Leipzig: Felix Meiner, 1918), p. 187.
2. Elie Halévy, *The Growth of Philosophical Radicalism* (Boston: Beacon Press, 1955; originally published in French, 1901-1904), p. 55.

penal law in the fourteenth century, Walter Ullman stated
that

> penological thought was still under the decisive influence of
> the retaliatory or retributive conception of punishment, un-
> mistakenly expressed in Roman law, which laid down that
> punishment is "noxae vindicta." Following this idea, the
> writing of the jurists abound in expressions...manifesting
> the retaliatory idea of punishment....Theological and
> canonistic research were also permeated with the retaliatory
> conception of punishment.... In accordance...the jurists
> laid stress on the postulate that punishment should be meted
> out according to the external wrong caused by the criminal.

That is why he found it exceptional that the Neapolitan
scholar Lucas de Penna (c.1320-c.1390) would formulate a
"theory of crime and punishment...far in advance of his
time" and showing "more than one fundamental
resemblance to the twentieth-century penological thought"
and anticipating "by four centuries the postulates of Beccaria, who was to submit his stirring ideas to a more respon-
sive public." Lucas claimed that the purpose of punishment
was to prevent future crime "by the moral improvement of
the offender . . . and by inculcating fear of punishment in
potential criminals,"[3] These views, out of tune with his times,
were in fact of ancient origin, and Lucas was merely reviving
ideas, already well expressed by ancient Greek philosophers
such as Socrates and Protagoras,[4] which would not effectively undermine the structure of retribution until the eighteenth
century. We find them well expressed in the works of two
men that would influence the thinking of the leaders of the
young American republic. One was William Blackstone,

---

3. Walter Ullman, *The Medieval Idea of Law,* as represented by Lucas de Penna
(New York: Barnes & Noble, 1969; originally published in 1946), pp. 142-143, 148.
4. See Introduction, *supra*.

whose *Commentaries on the Laws of England* (1765-1769) would become the guide for the adaptation of English law to the needs of the New World,[5] and the other was William Paley, whose *Principles of Moral and Political Philosphy* (1785) would for decades be the leading text on the subject in American colleges and universities. "As to the end or final cause of punishment," wrote Blackstone,

> this is not by way of atonement or expiation for the crime committed; for that must be left to the just determination of the Supreme Being; but as a prevention against future offenses of the same kind. This is effected three ways, either by the amendment of the offender himself...or by deterring others by the dread of his example...which gives rise to all ignominious punishments and to such executions of justice as are open and public, or lastly by depriving the party injuring of the power to do future mischief. Such is effected by either putting him to death or condemning him to perpetual confinement, slavery or exile.[6]

For Paley, "the proper end of human punishment is not the satisfaction of justice but the prevention of crimes. By the satisfaction of justice I mean the retribution of so much pain for so much guilt; which is the dispensation we expect at the

5. "Blackstone provided an admirably comprehensive, lucid and up-to-date systematization of the English common law suitable alike as a reference authority for the courts and as a text-book for students....This admirable systematization of the confused mass of English precedents exerted a profound influence upon the legal development of this country....It is hardly an exaggeration to say that what we actually took over from England was simply Blackstone." Julius S. Waterman, "Thomas Jefferson and Blackstone's Commentaries," *Illinois Law Review,* vol. 27, 1933, pp, 629-659; David A. Lockmiller, *Sir William Blackstone* (Chapel Hill: University of North Carolina Press, 1938), Chapter 10, "Blackstone in America."
6. *Commentaries on the Laws of England,* 4 vol. (Worcester, MA: Isaiah Thomas, 1790), vol. 4, pp. 11-12.

hand of God, and which we are accustomed to consider as the order of things that perfect justice dictates and requires." But the demand of justice that offenders be punished "is not the motive or occasion of human punishment.... . The fear lest the escape of the criminal should encourage him or others by his example to repeat the same crime, or to commit different crimes, is the sole consideration which authorizes the infliction of punishment by human laws.[7]

The belief that the death penalty is the supreme deterrent to murder is a hardy perennial deeply planted in the human mind and nourished by emotions. "No other punishment deters men so effectually from committing crimes as the punishment of death," wrote James Fitzjames Stephen in 1864.[8] He submitted that "this is one of those propositions which it is difficult to prove, simply because they are in themselves more obvious than any proof can make them. It is possible to display ingenuity in arguing against it, but that is all. The whole experience of mankind is in the other direction. The threat of instant death is the one to which resort has always been made when there was an absolute necessity for producing some result." Nevertheless, he felt compelled to offer proof and chose the most unconvincing one imaginable. "No one," he wrote, "goes to certain inevitable death except by compulsion.... . Was there ever yet a criminal who, when sentenced to death and brought out to die, would refuse the offer of a commutation of his sentence for the severest secondary punishment? Surely not. Why is this? It can only be because 'all that a man has will he give for his life.' " Lord Brentford, who was Home Secretary from 1924-1929, offered the same proof. "In all his five years' tenure of office he had only known one case in which the condemned man had been content to be hanged; in all the others the man and his family strove their utmost to save him from the gallows. That, to his

---

7. William Paley, *The Principles of Moral and Political Philosophy,* 9th ed. (Boston, 1818), pp. 339, 340.
8. "Capital Punishment," *Fraser's Magazine,* vol. 69, June, 1864, p. 753.

mind, was conclusive evidence of the value of the death penalty as a deterrent."[9] Both of these advocates seemed unaware of the difference between a potential danger and one that is imminent and seemingly inevitable. So was the Solicitor General of the United States in 1974, when he maintained that "the efforts of most criminals to avoid detection and to escape after being caught, show very clearly that they are sensitive to a calculus of pains and pleasures."[10] Surely, a murderer, for whom a possible death penalty had proved to be no deterrent, would be considered abnormal were he not to make every effort to escape death after being discovered and sentenced to die.

Stephen's belief that the deterrent power of the death penalty was self-evident has been shared by many. In a speech in the House of Lords in 1948, Lord Jowitt said that "to his mind there was only one possible justification of capital punishment — that its potency as a deterrent reduced the number of murders. He believed it did; he could not prove it; it must be a matter of impression and one's own personal opinion."[11] Lord Wright thought that deterrence "could obviously not be proved by evidence. It was a conclusion that must be drawn from 'the general impression one gains from experience, from looking around the world, from seeing how things are done and how people feel.' "[12] Lord Simon "had no doubt that capital punishment prevented more murders to an extent that no other punishment could. It was not a matter of statistics but of the judgment and common sense of every individual."[13] Lord Bridgeman based his belief in the deterrent force of the penalty "more on what I think is my

9. Sir Ernest Gowers, *A Life for a Life?* (London: Chatto & Windus, 1956), pp. 63-64. Gowers was chairman of the Royal Commission on Capital Punishment.
10. Robert H. Bork *et al., Brief for the United States as Amicus Curiae* in the Case of *Fowler* v. *North Carolina,* Supreme Court of the United States, October Term, 1974, p. 34.
11. Gowers, *op. cit.,* p. 54.
12. *Ibid.,* p. 56.
13. *Ibid.,* p. 62.

knowledge of human nature than anything else,"[14] and the Bishop of Truro thought that "on the value of the death penalty as a deterrent...his own feelings were a surer guide than any statistics from other countries...and he was sure that the death penalty would be a great deterrent to him if he were contemplating murder."[15]

It was on "evidence" of this character, anecdotal stories told by prison and police officials, and the firmly expressed beliefs of distinguished judicial witnesses, which led the Royal Commission on Capital Punishment in 1953 to conclude — cautiously — that

> *Prima facie* [i.e., common sense tells us] the penalty of death is likely to have a stronger effect as a deterrent to normal human beings than any other form of punishment, and there is some evidence (*though no convincing statistical evidence*) that this is in fact so. But this effect does not operate universally or uniformly, and there are many offenders on whom it is limited and may often be negligible. It is accordingly important to view this question in a just perspective and not to base a penal policy in relation to murder on exaggerated estimates of the uniquely deterrent force of the death penalty [emphasis added].[16]

Before arriving at this conclusion, the Commission had noted that "capital punishment has obviously failed as a deterrent when a murder is committed. We can number its failures. But we cannot number its successes. No one can ever know how many people have refrained from murder because of the fear of being hanged. For that we have to rely on indirect and inconclusive evidence."[17] The implication of this statement

14. *Ibid.*, p. 63.
15. *Ibid.*, pp. 51-52.
16. Royal Commission on Capital Punishment, 1949-1953, *Report* (London: Her Majesty's Stationery Office, September 1953). This remarkable report of 506 pages would contribute immensely to the debates, which finally led the British Parliament to abolish the death penalty for murder in 1965.
17. *Ibid.*, para. 59.

seems clear. The death penalty is assumed to be a deterrent, even though "no one can ever know," the evidence presumably remaining forever "inconclusive."

In recent years, the Supreme Court of the United States also has faced the problem of evaluating the deterrent force of the death penalty, but without arriving at a unanimous judgment. Its dominant view was given in the opinion delivered by Justice Stewart in the case of *Gregg* v. *Georgia*, July 2, 1976. He stated that studies of deterrence had been "inconclusive" and "although some...suggest that the death plenalty may not function as a significantly greater deterrent than lesser penalties, there is no convincing empirical evidence either supporting or refuting this view," and he quoted with approval the opinion of a legal scholar that "we do not know, and for systematic and visible reasons cannot know what the truth about this 'deterrent' effect may be.... A 'scientific' — that is to say, a soundly based — conclusion is simply impossible, and no methodological path out of this tangle suggests itself."[18]

One would naturally assume that after having declared that no one had been able to prove or could prove that the death penalty is a deterrent, the Court would have decided to avoid this issue altogether and focus its attention on other possible aims of the punishment, such as retribution or prevention. It did not. Indeed, in spite of its acknowledgment of the total absence of "convincing" evidence to support it, it affirmed that

> we may nevertheless assume safely that there are murderers, such as those who act in passion, for whom the threat of death has little or no deterrent effect. But for many others the death penalty undoubtedly is a significant deterrent. There are carefully contemplated murders, such as murder for hire,

---

18. Charles L. Black, Jr., *Capital Punishment: the Inevitability of Caprice and Mistake* (New York: W. W. Norton, 1974), pp. 25-26.

where the possible penalty of death may well enter into the cold calculus that precedes the decision to act. And there are some categories of murder, such as murder by a life prisoner, where other sactions may not be adequate.

What evidence was regarded as adequate to support these unexpected conclusions? Amazing as it may appear to serious students of the problem, the Court found it in the beliefs of legislators. "The value of capital punishment as a deterrent of crime is a complex factual issue the resolution of which properly rests with the legislatures, which can evaluate the results of statistical studies [though condemned by the Court as worthless] in terms of their own local conditions and with a flexibility of approach that is not available to the courts. . . . Indeed, many of the post-*Furman* statutes[19] reflect just such a responsible effort to define those crimes and those criminals for which capital punishment is most probably an effective deterrent." And in *Roberts* v. *Louisiana* (July 2, 1976) Justice White, speaking for the dissenting minority of the justices, accepted as proof of deterrence

the reasonable conclusions of Congress and 35 state legislatures that there are indeed certain circumstances in which the death penalty is the more efficacious deterrent of crime. It will not do to denigrate these legislative judgments as some form of vestigial savagery or as purely retributive in motivation; for they are solemn judgments, reasonably based, that imposition of the death penalty will save the lives of innocent persons. . . . A State should constitutionally be able to conclude that the need to deter some crimes and the likelihood that the death penalty will succeed in deterring these crimes is such that the death penalty may be made mandatory for all people who commit them.

---

19. In 1972, the Court had all but ourlawed capital punishment by its opinion in the case of *Furman* v. *Georgia*, resulting in a spate of capital legislation by states seeking to remedy the defects in their statutes, which had prompted the Court's action.

If we keep in mind that the issue is not the deterrent force of *punishment* but the claim that the *death penalty* is a more "efficacious deterrent of crime" than any other punishment, it is obvious that all the dogmatic assertions quoted above are simply personal opinions unsupported by any scientific evidence and based on intuition and common sense, which are untrustworthy guides in what the Court claimed to be uncharted territory. Common sense once upon a time told us that the earth was flat.

The "common sensers" should not be singled out for criticism in this connection, since even serious students of deterrence have been known to advance even stranger arguments in support of punishment. Two examples will suffice. They do not specifically deal with capital punishment but we can be certain that a search of the literature on the death penalty would uncover a similar argument pertaining to that punishment. "Does anyone...seriously maintain that the incidence of crime would not rise in the total absence of legal sanctions? If we abolish all penalties for theft, theft will not increase?"[20] Or, "let us imagine a fictitious city which has a million adult male inhabitants, who commit a hundred rapes annually. Suppose, then, that abolishing the crime of rape led to an increase in the number of rape cases to one thousand.... From the viewpoint of the legal machinery...the increase in rape had demonstrated the tremendous importance of general prevention."[21]

These arguments are non sequiturs and therefore nonsensical. Neither "theft" nor "rape" could increase or decrease if they are no longer crimes. Taking property from someone without his permission or forcing a woman to have sexual intercourse would occur and might even become common

---

20. Richard L. Henshel, "Considerations, Deterrence and System Capacity Models," *Criminology,* vol. 16, May 1978, pp. 35-46; p.40.
21. Johannes Andenaes, *Punishment and Deterrence* (Ann Arbor: University of Michigan Press, 1974), p. 44.

events, but this would either be considered normal conduct or be subjected to controls in which the "legal machinery" might not have any role to play.

It is obvious that, in spite of the pessimism voiced by Professor Black in the quotation cited earlier, we must persevere in the attempt to discover if the common-sense view of the deterrent power of the death penalty can be justified by facts other than the mere proof that the belief is widely held. Does this punishment in fact deter potential murderers, leaving aside the question of whether it does so more effectively than would some other punishment, such as imprisonment for life or a long term of years? The search for conclusive evidence permitting a positive or negative answer to this question has been pursued off and on ever since Cesare Beccaria in 1764 claimed that the death penalty was not deterrent and should therefore be abolished and replaced by a punishment that would really possess that force.[22]

The study of the moralizing effect of capital punishment on the population at large requires an understanding or agreement on what general deterrence means and how it is supposed to operate through the threat or application of the penalty of death. In a lengthy report on "The Death Penalty and the Problem of Deterrence," requested by the Royal Commission on Capital Punishment in 1951, I attempted to define the matter.

> The process of deterrence is obviously a psychological one. It presumes in this connection that life is regarded by man as a precious possession which he wishes to preserve more eagerly, perhaps, than any other of his attributes. He would therefore defend it to the utmost against every threat, including the threat of capital execution. Every such threat, it is assumed, arouses his fear and as a rational being he would try to con-

---

22. *Dei delitti e delle pene.* The relevant chapter of this important work, "Of Crimes and of Punishments," is translated in Thorsten Sellin, ed., *Capital Punishment* (New York: Harper & Row, 1967), pp. 39–45.

duct himself in such a manner that the threat would be avoided or that, once materialized, it would be nullified. It is further assumed that the potential threat is made vivid to him by the fact that he knows that the death penalty exists.

If the death penalty carries a potential threat, which has a restraining influence on human conduct, we may assume that the greater the threat the more effective it would be. Now, the term "death penalty" as used in discussions concerning its deterrent power may mean many things. First we have the death penalty defined by law as a mandatory or discretionary punishment for crime. Then we have the death penalty that looms as a possible threat to a person arrested for, or accused of a capital offense, and the death penalty pronounced but not yet executed. Finally, we have the death penalty actually applied to the offender. Presumably, the potential power of deterrence of the death penalty is not the same at all these levels of manifestation. Were it present in the law alone, it would be completely robbed of its threat.... We arrive then at the conclusion that if the death penalty is to have any restraining effect there must be *an adequate threat of execution*, but no one has ventured to calculate how great the risk of possible execution must be in order to constitute an adequate threat.[23]

This statement implies that there is need for research that would determine (1) the effect of arrests, prosecutions, convictions, and executions for capital murder on the incidence, in a population, of murders and especially of murderers, who represent the negative effects of deterrence; their relative number may be expected to decline if general deterrence operates as its advocates believe it does; (2) the effect of the abolition or introduction of capital punishment by the state on the incidence of murders and murderers in the population. Furthermore, (3) the claims that the lives of police are safer in death penalty states than in abolitionist states, or that the

---

23. Royal Commission on Capital Punishment, *Minutes of Evidence,* Thirtieth Day, Thursday, 1st February, 1951, p. 648.

threat of capital punishment is especially effective in staying the hand of potential murderers in the population of penal institutions can be tested by research, and (4) the likelihood that murderers, who are paroled or otherwise released from prison, would kill again can also be determined by research that would allay or justify the commonly held fear that this would occur.

The utility of such research in furnishing a sound basis for legislation on capital punishment has in recent years been increasingly questioned by many competent students of deterrence, who are well represented on the Panel on Research on Deterrent and Incapacitative Effects of the Committee on Research on Law Enforcement and Criminal Justice of the National Research Council's Assembly of Behavioral and Social Sciences. In a report issued in 1978,[24] the Panel did suggest that "if research on capital punishment is pursued, adequate base-line data establishing the recent trends in capital crime should be collected and attempts should be made to discriminate among the various manifestations of the capital punishment threat, including the probability of execution given homicide, the rate of capital sentences or executions per year and the media coverage of capital sentences or executions." These suggestions would seem futile gestures because the Panel thought that if public policy on sanctions were to be based on research on the deterrent force of the death penalty "extremely severe standards of proof" would be required, and that "non-experimental research, to which the study of the deterrent effects of capital punishment is necessarily limited, almost certainly will be unable to meet those standards of proof." Therefore, "research on this topic is not likely to produce findings that will or should [!] have much influence on policy makers."[25]

---

24. Albert Blumstein, Jacqueline Cohen, and Daniel Nagin, eds., *Deterrence and Incapacitation: Estimating the Effects of Criminal Sanctions on Crime Rates* (Washington, DC: National Academy of Sciences, 1978), pp. 3-63.
25. *Ibid.*, p. 63.

A part of this judgment is realistic, since in the battle between reason and emotions, the latter tend to prevail, verifying David Hume's claim that reason is the slave of passions. In my memorandum to the Royal Commission on Capital Punishment in 1951, the concluding paragraph read as follows:

> The question of whether the death penalty is to be dropped, retained or instituted is not dependent on the evidence as to its utilitarian effects, but on the strength of popular beliefs and sentiments not easily influenced by such evidence. These beliefs and sentiments have their roots in a people's culture. They are conditioned by a multitude of factors, such as the character of social institutions, social, economic and political ideas, etc. If at a given time such beliefs and sentiments become so oriented that they favour the abolition of the death penalty, facts like those presented in this paper will be acceptable as evidence, but are likely to be as quickly ignored if social changes provoke resurgence of the old sentiments. When a people no longer *likes* the death penalty for murderers it will be removed no matter what may happen to the homicide rates. This is what has happened in the past in connection with crimes against property.[26]

This circumstance must not close the door on research on the effects of the death penalty on the incidence and trend of murder, as intimated by the Panel. Even if the findings of such research do not meet the "extremely severe standards of proof" that would render them absolutely unassailable, they can — like straws in the wind that show the general direction of an atmospheric disturbance but do not measure its velocity or direction perfectly — furnish policy makers with facts that point to the general nature of the issue and the probable answers to the questions it raises. Were legislators to wait to

---

26. Royal Commission on Capital Punishment, *Minutes of Evidence,* Thirtieth Day, Thursday, 1st February, 1951, p. 656.

act on all-important social issues until they possessed absolute knowledge of their dimensions and of the outcome of their own decisions, legislation would reach a standstill.

Chapter 6

THE POLICE AND THE DEATH PENALTY

The proverbial "man in the street" believes that the death penalty should be retained. This seems to be the message of opinion polls today. This sentiment is not always crystallized in resolutions adopted by organized groups, except when legislative bodies contemplate the possibility of abolishing this punishment. Then organizations consisting of personnel engaged in law enforcement and the administration of justice tend to voice their opposition. The most vocal of such groups is the police, who regard the threat of execution that faces a potential murderer to be a powerful shield protecting them in the exercise of their hazardous duties. A good example is the view expressed in 1954 by the president of the Chief Constables' Association of Canada to a parliamentary committee studying capital punishment.

> I feel I am quite correct in saying that we of the police service are not in favour of the death penalty for murder being abolished, because there is no doubt in our minds that it does act as a deterrent. Our main objection is that abolition would adversely affect the personal safety of police officers in the daily discharge of their duties. We are the people who have to apprehend persons suspected of having committed violent and vicious crimes, persons perhaps who have already taken

the life of another human being. It would be interesting to
know, and if time had permitted I would have tried to obtain
this vital information as to the number of policemen
murdered in the execution of their duty in those parts of the
world where capital punishment has been abolished. I submit
that it will be found the number is much higher than in those
countries where the death penalty is still in effect, and this
point is the main one in our submission that our government
should retain capital punishment as a form of security.[1]

This statement did not only express a belief that police are
more likely to be killed by criminals in abolitionist than in
retentionist states; it showed a blind belief unsupported by
facts. Finally, it implied that if studies would prove the belief
without foundation, the police would lose its principal argument in favor of capital punishment. What a challenge to a
researcher! Especially as no investigation testing the validity
of the claim could be found in the volumunious literature on
the death penalty. Two studies were promptly begun, one
focusing on municipal police forces in the six abolition states
of Maine, Michigan, Minnesota, North Dakota, Rhode
Island, and Wisconsin and the eleven retentionist states contiguous to them: Connecticut, Illinois, Indiana, Iowa,
Masachusetts, Montana, New Hampshire, New York, Ohio,
South Dakota, and Vermont. The other dealt with state
police forces in twenty-four of twenty-seven states having
such agencies.[2]

---

1. Walter H. Mulligan in *Minutes of Proceedings and Evidence* of the Joint Committee of the Senate and the House of Commons on Capital and Corporal Punishment and Lotteries, no. 8, April 27, 1954 (Ottawa: Queen's Printer).
2. Thorsten Sellin, "The Death Penalty and Police Safety," *Minutes of Proceedings and Evidence,* no. 20 (Ottawa: Queen's Printer, 1955), Appendix F, pp.
718-728. Reprinted in Hugo Adam Bedau, ed., *The Death Penalty in America*
(Garden City, NY: Anchor Books, 1964) and in Thorsten Sellin, ed., *Capital
Punishment* (New York: Harper & Row, 1967); Donald R. Campion, S.J., "The
State Police and the Death Penalty," *Minutes of Proceedings and Evidence,* no. 20,
pp. 729-741. Reprinted in Bedau, *op. cit.*

The results of the first of these studies were derived from replies to a questionnaire sent to all police departments in 593 cities with a population of at least 10,000 in 1950. Information was requested, year by year, for the period 1919-1954, on the number of police officers killed "by a lethal weapon in the hands of a criminal or a suspect." Usable replies were received from 55 percent of the cities in the abolitionist states and from 41 percent of the cities in retentionist states. The findings are shown in Table 6.1. A different look at the problem is made possible by Table 6.2, which compares police homicide rates for smaller cities which supplied the largest number of reports. Only the states with at least 10 cities with 10,000-30,000 inhabitants in 1950 were rated. Neither table lends support to the claim that the police are safer in death penalty states. Nor does the rate of police killed in Chicago compared with the rate for Detroit yield a different conclusion. These cities had rates of .015 and .014, respectively, covering the period 1928-1948.

Table 6.1: Comparative Rates of Police Killed in Selected States, 1919-1954

Population in Thousands		Rate, per 100,000 of Population in These Cities, 1950			
		Abolition States		Retentionist States	
10-30	(186)	1.3	(61)	1.2	(125)
30-60	(52)	1.0	(15)	1.1	(37)
60-100	(13)	1.6	(4)	1.0	(9)
100-350	(11)	.6	(1)	1.5	(10)
500-650	(3)	.8	(1)	1.9	(2)
Total	(265)	1.2	(82)	1.3	(183)

NOTE: Number of cities in parentheses.

Table 6.2: Police Homicide Rates in Cities of 10,000-30,000 Inhabitants, 1950

Abolition States	(61)		Retentionist States	(125)	
Michigan	(24)	1.9	Ohio	(21)	1.9
Minnesota	(14)	1.5	Illinois	(14)	1.9
Wisconsin	(13)	.9	Indiana	(10)	1.7
			Massachusetts	(31)	1.2
			New York	(24)	.7
			Connecticut	(11)	.0
Total		1.3	Total		1.2

NOTE: Number of cities in parentheses.

Father Campion's state police study was based on the same questionnaire used in the research reported above, but he faced a problem arising from the fact that not all the twenty-four agencies had been in existence during the same span of years. The state police of Connecticut and Pennsylvania supplied data for 1903-1954, while the California Highway Patrol could do so for 1946-1954 only. Altogether, the reports from the six abolition states covered a total of 158 years; from the eighteen retentionist states, 494 years.[3] There were 71 officers killed in the death penalty states, 6 in the rest. An average of 26 years separated the police homicides in the abolition states, but in the retentionist states they occurred, on the average, every 7 years. Under these circumstances, the conclusion of the author that the data available to him did "not lend empirical support to the claim that the existence of the death penalty in the statutes of a state provides a greater pro-

---

3. California, Connecticut, Georgia, Illinois, Indiana, Iowa, Maryland, Massachusetts, Missouri, Nebraska, Yew York, Ohio, Oregon, Pennsylvania, South Dakota, Texas, Washington, and West Virginia.

tection to the police than exists in states where that penalty has been abolished'' seems amply justified.

One procedure in Sellin's study could be questioned, namely, the use of comparative rates based on the population of the specific cities in the abolitionist and the retentionist states, instead of basing them on the population at risk, i.e., the police forces of these cities. The effect of this choice will be seen when we examine the findings of some later studies. The use of the 1950 census to establish the population base for the rates might be questioned too. ''It might be argued,'' wrote the author,

> that it is improper to use the 1950 population as the base for the computation of rates that involve cases scattered over a thirty-six year period preceding [and following]. It would undoubtedly be possible to arrive at some population figure which would on the surface appear more defensible, but which would on close analysis be found to have equally great defects, for it must be remembered that all the cities involved have undergone the effect of considerable migratory changes due to a depression and a world war and that no one can determine with any real accuracy what population basis is preferable. It is believed that the rates reflect with reasonable faithfulness the comparative size of the problem in the different states and in the two types of states.[4]

Between 1920 and 1950 the urban population of the abolitionist states increased by 74 percent and that of the retentionist states by 50 percent. Since the cities studies probably increased at the same rates, it seems reasonable to assume that this growth would not change the *relative* rates of the police homicides.

In connection with the assembling of the data on ''crimes known'' for analysis and publication in the *Uniform Crime Reports*, the statistical section of the Federal Bureau of In-

---

4. Sellin, ''The Death Penalty and Police Safety,'' op. cit., p. 722.

vestigation began in 1957 to call for information from the cooperating police agencies on the number of police killed, feloniously or accidentally. Within a few years the Bureau was receiving this information on individual forms. Copies of these reports were generously supplied to the author for the years 1961-1963 and 1964-1966 and subjected to analysis.[5] The main findings for the earlier period are summarized in Table 6.3, which shows that there were 9 police killed feloniously in the abolitionist states of Michigan (2), Minnesota (2), North Dakota (1), and Wisconsin (4); none in Maine or Rhode Island. In six of the nine contiguous retentionist states 21 officers were slain: in Massachusetts (4), Connecticut (1), Ohio (5), Indiana (4), Illinois (4), and Iowa (3); none in New Hampshire, South Dakota, or Montana. The rates of police killed in the two classes of states are remarkably similar.

Table 6.3: Rates of Police Killed, 1961-1963

	Number Killed	Rate per 1,000 Police	Rate per Million Population (1960 Census)
Abolitionist States	9	.393	.510
Retentionist States	21	.398	.570

5. Albert P. Cardarelli, "An Analysis of Police Killed by Criminal Action: 1961-1963," *Journal of Criminal Law, Criminology and Police Science,* vol. 59, September 1968, pp. 447-453; Robert A. Silverman, "An Analysis of Police Killed in the United States 1964-1966," unpublished paper for criminological seminar, University of Pennsylvania, Spring 1968. We were indebted to Mr. Jerome J. Daunt, Chief of the Uniform Crime Reporting Section of the FBI for his assistance.

A slightly different result is shown for the 1964-1966 period. During those years 12 officers were killed in the abolitionist states: Maine (3), Michigan (4), Minnesota (4), and Wisconsin (1). North Dakota and Rhode Island reported none killed. In the contiguous retentionist states Massachusetts, New Hampshire, Iowa, and Montana had no slayings, but there were 17 in Connecticut (1), Ohio (5), Indiana (6), Illinois (4), and South Dakota (1). The risk rate per 1000 police was .17 in the abolitionist states and .11 in the retentionist ones. This finding, seemingly supporting the claim that the death penalty does act as a deterrent, led Silverman to examine the situation in the country as a whole, because in addition to the 17 cases already mentioned there were 131 police killed in the rest of the retentionist states.

Table 6.4 distributes the slain officers in retentionist states by area of the country and shows that the highest risk police ran of being feloniously killed was in the South, which also displayed the highest rate of willful homicides and most of the capital executions during the period. The New England region of the Northeast area had the lowest rate (.021), the lowest willful homicide rate (19.8), and no executions. The highest risk rates were those of Wyoming (1.626), a death penalty state, and Alaska (1.437), an abolitionist one. The lowest were found in Wisconsin (.064), abolitionist, and in the death penalty states of New York (.076), and Illinois (.077).

In recent years, the *Uniform Crime Report,* published by the Federal Bureau of Investigation annually, has included extensive information on police killed feloniously and has also listed, by locality, the size of police forces in states, cities, and counties. The annual report for 1975 and a special summary report for that year have been chosen at random for analysis for the purpose of determining if police are less likely

Table 6.4: Risk Rates, Willful Homicide Rates, and Executions in Death Penalty States, 1964-1966

Area	Number Police Killed	Risk Rate per 1,000 Police[a]	Crude Homicide Rate per Million Population[b]	Number of Executions[c]
Northeast	22	.087	35.3	0
North Central	20	.144	38.5	7
South	80	.434	82.0	14
West	26	.222	41.3	2
Total	148	.212	57.7	23

NOTE: Based on Tables 2, 3, 20 and 21 of Silverman's report. In addition to the states that were already abolitionist in 1964, he excluded five states that abolished capital punishment at some time during the period. There were 18 police killed in those states. Also excluded was the case of a police officer killed in Guam.

a. "Size of force at risk was computed by summing the number of male government police, marshals and sheriffs listed by the Census Bureau for 1960."
b. Based on census estimates of population during the period, and on number of murders and non negligent manslaughters reported in the annual *Uniform Crime Reports* of the FBI.
c. See Table 2 of the *National Prisoner Statistics: Executions, 1930-1960*, no. 41 (Washington, DC: U.S. Department of Justice, Bureau of Prisons, April 1967).

to be killed in retentionist states than in those states where the death penalty has been eliminated.[6]

6. *Crime in the United States, 1975, Uniform Crime Reports for the United States* (Washington, DC: Federal Bureau of Investigation, 1976); U.S. Department of Justice, *Law Enforcement Officers Killed, Summary 1975* (Washington, DC: Federal Bureau of Investigation, 1976).

The *Summary* tabulated, by state and locality within the state, the police killed during the year, unless a state or highway patrol officer was the victim, in which case the locality was not specified. Case histories of the slayings were also included in the report. The annual report, on the other hand, gave (in its Table 74), the number of full-time state police and highway patrol officers in each state, and in other tables (75 and 76), by state, the number of police employees in each city with populations of (1) 25,000 or higher and (2) under 25,000. Tables 78 and 79 gave the same data for (1) suburban counties and (2) rural counties with more than 25,000 population. For the larger cities police officers, by sex, were tabulated separately from civilian employees, but otherwise only the number of "police employees," by sex, were counted. On the basis of these tables and the tabulations and case histories of the *Summary*, Table 6.5 has been constructed. It compares the risk of police being killed in abolitionist and retentionist states. The rates are based on the total number of police in each area and category of population groups and not on the police forces in the specific localities where the killings occurred, the assumption being that the exposure to risk is general and not specific. The table shows that the risk rates was usually lower in the abolitionist states, one glaring exception being in the area of the South, which had only one such state, West Virginia, where three killings occurred, its risk rate being twice that of the rest of the South. In the North Central area both classes of states had identical rates. It is noteworthy that all the state and highway police were killed in death penalty states.

Not only did the police in retentionist states run a greater risk of being feloniously killed, but so did the slayers and suspects involved in these homicides. The *Summary*'s case histories of these slayings give the number of active or passive participants involved, the number arrested, and the number killed by the police, as well as the number who eluded arrest

Table 6.5: Comparative Rates of Risk of Police Being Slain: Continental United States, 1975 (A = Abolitionist States; R = Retentionist States; Risk Rate = Rate per 1000 Police)

| | Cities with Populations of | | | | Suburban and Rural Counties | | State Police and Highway Patrolmen | | Total[a] | |
| | 25,000 or more | | under 25,000 | | | | | | | |
Area	A	R	A	R	A	R	A	R	A	R
Northeast										
Police Killed	1	10	1	3	1	2	—	1	3	16
Risk Rate	.088	.149	.102	.177	.102	.187	—	.103	.090	.153
North Central										
Police Killed	3	10	3	2	2	3	—	—	8	15
Risk Rate	.165	.267	.365	.119	.317	.365	—	—	.221	.220
South										
Police Killed	—	17	1	12	2	14	—	7	3	50
Risk Rate	—	.308	1.076	.464	4.073	.594	—	.510	1.191	.520
West										
Police Killed	1	7	—	5	1	4	—	3	2	19
Risk Rate	.197	.219	—	.558	.293	.129	—	.367	.147	.237
Total										
Number of Police	35,167	182,641	21,696	68,585	19,984	69,486	8,561	37,179	85,408	357,891
Police Killed	5	44	5	22	6	23	—	11	16	100
Risk Rate	.142	.241	.230	.321	.300	.331	—	.296	.187	.279

Table 6.5 (continued)

NOTE: The 1975 *Summary* report listed 129 killings, omitting 1 in Guam described in one of the case histories of the report. Of the 129, however, 1 occurred in the Virgin Islands and 6 in Puerto Rico, leaving 122 occurring in the continental United States. However, only 116 are included in this table, because the sizes of the police forces of which they were members were not given in the cases of four federal agents of unspecified forces, one Navajo tribal policeman in Arizona, and one Bureau of Indian Affairs employee in Colorado — both killed in retributionist states.

b. No police officer was killed in the abolitionist states of Hawaii, Iowa, Maine, Minnesota, North Dakota, Rhode Island, or Washington nor in the death penalty states of Connecticut, Delaware, Idaho, Montana, Nebraska, New Mexico, New Hampshire, South Dakota, Utah, Vermont, or Wyoming.

by committing suicide and the number who escaped it by flight. These are found in Table 6.6, which shows that of the individuals the police successfully disposed of in retentionist states, 1 out of 5 was either killed by the police or killed themselves, compared with 7.4 percent in the abolitionist states — i.e., 1 killed in Michigan and 1 in West Virginia. One might say that when the victims of homicide were police officers, spontaneous "unofficial executions" took place. This represents, of course, only a small proportion of the criminals who were killed in the United States while attempting or committing a homicide, or immediately afterward. A dramatic illustration is furnished by Chicago for the years 1933-1954, when policemen killed 69 (21 percent) and private citizens 261 (79 percent) persons involved in homicide (a total of 330). The risk which homicidal offenders ran of losing their lives at the hands of police or private citizens was eight times greater than the risk of being placed in the electric chair at the Cook County Jail, where 45 persons were executed after being convicted of capital murder. "There were 5,132 murders and non-negligent manslaughters known to the police during these years. In connection with 6.45 percent of these homicides, a criminal or suspect met his death at the hands of police or citizens, while .88 percent were put to death in the electric chair."[7] If the fear of death stops people from committing murder, it is the prospect of being killed at the scene of the crime which should be the greater deterrent rather than the prospect of being officially executed at some time in the future, yet this factor is never alluded to by the advocates of deterrence.

The data presented in these pages permit only one conclusion, namely, that the belief of the police that in order to be safer in their occupation they need laws that threaten potential murderers with death has no factual basis. Indeed, it is

7. Thorsten Sellin, *The Death Penalty* (Philadelphia: American Law Institute, 1959), p. 62.

Table 6.6: Killers of Police in the Continental United States, 1975

Area	Arrest	Disposed of by Killing	% Killed	Escaped Arrest	Suicides	Total
Retentionist States						
Northeast	19	3	13.6	3	—	25
North Central	16	2	11.1	3	—	21
South	54	12	18.2	4	4	74
West	18	2	10.0	3	3	26
Total	107	19	15.1	13	7	146
Abolitionist States						
Northeast	4	—	—	—	—	4
North Central	14	1	6.7	—	—	15
South	4	1	20.0	—	—	5
West	3	—	—	—	—	3
Total	25	2	7.4	—	—	27
Grand Total	132	23	14.8	13	7	173

evident that the police are more efficient executioners than the public hangman and should inspire more fear than any capital law could do if deterrence were operative.

It is natural that the police in states that have traditionally supported the death penalty should share popular beliefs in its deterrent power, but their occupation as guardians of the law lends additional force to that belief, for they are constantly placed in situations in which they confront persons engaged in illicit conduct who may use even deadly force to facilitate their escape. It is the danger of death inflicted by personal adversaries that distinguishes this occupational hazard from the accidental deaths caused by impersonal agents and suffered by workers in many occupations more dangerous to life than is police work. We have noted that in

1975, for instance, the risk of police being feloniously killed was at the rate of .262 per thousand. During the 1972-1976 period the average accidental death rate for anthracite miners working underground was 1.250 per thousand.

Chapter 7

THE RECIDIVISM OF
CAPITAL MURDERERS

Supporters of the death penalty claim that this punishment is a superior means of saving lives, because if a capital murderer were sentenced to life imprisonment, he may some day kill a fellow prisoner or member of the prison staff, the assumption being that he is, more than a prisoner sentenced for some other crime, prone to homicidal violence; and, if at some future time he were pardoned, paroled, or otherwise released from confinement, this presumed propensity might lead him to kill again. In either case, these conceivable dangers would not exist if he had been executed in the first place.

These suppositions seem reasonable. Homicides do occur inside prisons now and then and some paroled or discharged prisoners have been known to commit murder, but to test the validity of the suppositions we need to know if such homicides were perpetrated by prisoners serving sentences for *capital* murder or free after serving a part of such sentences. Therefore, we are not primarily concerned with those convicted of second-degree murder or voluntary manslaughter, which the law does not regard as capital crimes. For them, the above suppositions are inapplicable. However, since the crimes of capital and other murderers are so often similar and their final classification so frequently due to fortuitous decisions by prosecutors and juries, the recidivism of second-degree murderers cannot be ignored.

The Imprisoned Murderer

Our first concern is with the conduct of prisoners who are serving sentences for murder. Are these offenders a special threat to the lives of their fellow prisoners or members of the staff of the institution in which they are confined? One might assume that it would not be difficult to locate information which would supply an answer to that question. Surely, a murder committed in a prison would be given attention in the annual report of the warden or the state board of corrections. Not so. The student of these documents would rarely learn anything about the observance of the rules of the institution by the prisoners or their infractions of the criminal law. Prison administrators do not dwell in their reports on the seamy side of prison life. If the report should happen to contain more than a cursory notice of the activities of the prison physician, one might learn, for instance, that he treated some inmate or guard for stab wounds that proved fatal; this would be about all that could be gleaned from official reports except when a riot has occurred and a special investigation into its scope and causes is conducted.

It is also idle to seek an answer to the question in general studies of homicide. Not even a hint is found in H. C. Brearley's *Homicide in the United States*. In an extensive study of criminal homicide in California dealing with all such crimes reported in 1960, seven cases that occurred in the prisons of the state were included but not separately examined.[1] In other words, to elicit the data we need one must consult researches that have been designed specifically for the

---

1. H. C. Brearley, *Homicide in the United States* (Chapel Hill: University of North Carolina Press, 1932); Romney P. Narloch, *Criminal Homicide in California: a Cohort Study* (Sacramento: Bureau of Criminal Statistics, n.d.).

purpose of finding the answer to the question posed earlier. Such studies are extremely rare. Indeed, the first ones were made by the author based on data secured from American prisons for the years 1964 and 1965. Before examining their findings, however, something should be said about the setting in which prison homicides occur.

Anyone who has studied prisons and especially the maximum-security institutions, which are the most likely abodes of murderers serving sentences of life imprisonment or long terms of years, realizes that the society of captives within their walls is subject to extraordinary strains and pressures, which most of those in the outside world experience in attenuated forms, if at all. The prison is an unnatural institution. In an area of limited size, surrounded by secure walls, it houses from a few score to several thousand inmates and their custodians. In this unisexual agglomeration of people, separated from family and friends, prisoners are constantly thrown into association with one another and subject to a host of regulations that limit their freedom of action and are imposed partly by the prison authorities and partly by the inmate code. It is not astonishing that in this artificial environment altercations occur, bred by the clash of personalities and the conflict of interests that lead to fights in free society, especially when one considers that most of the maximum-security prison inmates are fairly young and have been raised in the poorer quarters of our cities, where resort to physical violence in the settlement of disputes is common. Indeed, what surprises the student of prison violence is the relative rarity of assaultive events, everything considered. For instance, during the twelve months preceding October 1973, the average daily population of inmates in the state prisons of New York was close to 13,000. There were only 197 known serious assaults by inmates on inmates and 119 by inmates on officers. There were no fatalities.[2]

---

2. *Annual Report, New York State Department of Correctional Services* (Albany, 1974), p. 35.

Early in 1965 a questionnaire was sent to the federal Bureau of Prisons and all state prison administrations requesting information on homicides occurring in their prisons during 1964. Replies were received from 41 of the 50 states, the federal Bureau, and the District of Columbia. Of the jurisdictions failing to report, the most important were Florida, Louisiana, Maryland, and New York.

A total of 3 homicides were committed in federal prisons and 28 in institutions of 15 of the reporting states; the latter occurred in Alabama (3), California (5), Colorado (2), Georgia (3), Indiana (1), Iowa (1), Michigan (2), Mississippi (1), North Carolina (1), Ohio (1), Pennsylvania (2), Texas (1), Virginia (2), Washington (1), and West Virginia (2). All the victims were convicts and, save in one unsolved case, 32 convicts were identified as the killers.

All the above jurisdictions, except Michigan, had the death penalty, and over the previous 35 years most of them had applied it frequently to convicted murderers. During the preceding year, 1963, 10 of the 18 executions for murder occurred in California (1), Georgia (2), Mississippi (2), Ohio (2), Texas (2), and Washington (1).

The two killers in Michigan were serving time for manslaughter and unarmed robbery, respectively. In Ohio, next door, and in Mississippi, the killers were serving life for capital murder. In the North Carolina case and in one of the Pennsylvania events, the killer was in prison for life for non-capital murder. In other words, five of the 32 offenders were already serving time for some degree of homicide. Eleven others were in prison for robbery (9), kidnapping (1), and one under a life sentence for being a habitual criminal. The three convicts who died in Georgia met their deaths at the hands of two men, one of whom was serving life and the other awaiting execution for armed robbery. Since it is quite possible that the "habitual criminal" was a property offender, at least fifteen of the killers were in prison for crimes of violence against the person. Sixteen were definitely serving sentences for property crimes — six for burglary, four for theft, five for some narcotics offense, and one for forgery.[3]

A similar inquiry, covering the year 1965, was undertaken by the author a year later. Data were reported from forty-five states, the District of Columbia, and the federal system. Five states, Alabama, Arizona, Arkansas, Idaho, and Maine failed to respond. Part of the succinct report on this research will be reproduced verbatim in subsequent pages.[4]

Sixty-one persons were killed in the institutions. Eight staff members were among the victims. Of the fifty-three convicts killed, nine were slain by unidentified persons in death-penalty states. Four of these "anonymous" homicides occurred in California, two in the federal prison at Leavenworth, Kansas, and one each in the Indiana State Prison, the Georgia State Prison, and the Walpole Prison in Massachusetts. Two of the killings resulted from racial conflicts and one from an unpaid debt. Three of the California victims were Youth Authority wards and the fourth was said to be a former Nazi leader. The Indiana victim, a mental case, was struck by a chair, and although many witnessed the assault, the inmate code protected the assailant.

The remaining 52 victims were killed in 46 events, in which 59 convicts were identified as assailants. These incidents occurred in 23 states and the federal system, all death-penalty jurisdictions except Hawaii, Iowa, Michigan, and Minnesota. In 2 cases a prisoner killed more than 1 person. At the Fort Pillow State Farm, Tennessee, an inmate serving a three-year term for third-degree burglary and petty larceny killed a security guard and a fellow inmate, and in the Virginia State Penitentiary a prisoner serving a double life term for robbery and murder killed the assistant superintendent and a prison

---

3. The fullest report on this study is found in Thorsten Sellin, "Homicides and Serious Assaults in Prisons," Aristotelian University of Tessaloniki, *Annual of the School of Law and Economics,* vol. 14, 1966, pp. 139-145.
4. Thorsten Sellin, "Prison Homicides," in Thorsten Sellin, ed., *Capital Punishment* (New York: Harper & Row, 1967), pp. 154-160.

physician. On the other hand, in 7 events, 2 or more
assailants and 1 or more victims were involved — 20 offenders and 11 victims in all. The most serious occurred in
Hawaii, an abolitionist state, and in Illinois. The state
prison's yard was the scene of the Hawaii incident. Five
prisoners suspected of belonging to a faction trying to smug-
gle barbiturates into the institution engaged in a gang fight
armed with two smuggled pistols and two knives. One of the
participants, serving a ten-year sentence for assault with a
deadly weapon was fatally stabbed by a car thief serving a
five-year sentence; he was, in turn, shot by a tower guard.
Another participant, a burglar serving a sentence of twenty
years, was killed, and two others, a convict serving twenty
years for attempted murder and one serving forty years for
robbery, were charged with the crime.

The Illinois affray occurred at the Menard Prison in connection with a riot that began in the dining hall. Before it ended two lieutenants and a guard had been stabbed to death and
a steward and five guards wounded, three seriously. Charged
with these homicides were a murderer serving a sentence of 25
years, a thief serving three to seven years, a forger serving
three to ten years, and an armed robber serving three to five
years.

In the Georgia State Prison two inmates, one serving 20
years for voluntary murder and the other 4 to 10 years for
assault to murder, killed an inmate in revenge arising from a
struggle between rival cliques. Two inmates of the Kansas
State Penitentiary — one serving sentences of 20 to 42 years
and life, respectively, for robbery and murder, and one serving 1 to 5 years for grand larceny — killed an inmate as a
result of a sex affair. In the Minnesota State Reformatory,
two inmates serving a 5-year term for burglary and a 40-year
term for robbery, respectively, armed with a butcher knife
and a cleaver, attacked three inmates, killing one of them. In
the Missouri State Penitentiary, two robbers serving 10 and
15 years killed a fellow prisoner in revenge; and at San Quen-

tin, three prisoners — two robbers serving 5 years to life and a prisoner serving 1 year to life for a previous assault in prison — killed an inmate during a fight arising from pressure brought on the victim to sell his drug business.

Six of the eight staff members killed figure in the above events. In addition, a San Quentin convict serving a sentence of 5 years to life for selling narcotics stabbed a shop foreman during a disciplinary action; and in an unidentified Pennsylvania prison a convict described as a mental case and serving a 30-to-60-year term for aggravated robbery, killed a sergeant for no known reason.

Altogether, the 59 assailants were at the time serving sentences for

Murder	16	Burglary	4
Manslaughter	1	Theft	7
Assault to murder	2	Selling narcotics	1
Rape	1	Dyer Act violation	2
Assault	3	Possessing sawed-off	1
Kidnapping	1	shotgun	
Robbery	19	Delinquency	1

The striking feature of this tabulation is that 43 of the 59 killers were in prison for crimes of violence against the person. Robbers formed the largest group, followed by convicts serving terms for some form of homicide, 16 of them for murder, but only 11 of these for capital murder punishable by death — 4 in Louisiana, and 1 each in Georgia, Illinois, Indiana, Kansas, South Carolina, Texas, and Virginia. Of the remaining 5, 2 were in prison in abolitionist states, Iowa and Michigan, and 3 were serving terms for second-degree, i.e., noncapital, murder in California, Nebraska, and North Carolina.

Nine of the convicts were serving time for some capital crime other than murder — one for assault to murder in Georgia, one for rape in Louisiana, two for armed robbery in Missouri, four for robbery in Virginia, and one for the federal crime of kidnapping.

Could the lives of the victims of these homicides have been saved? It is obvious that if the 11 convict killers had been sentenced to death and executed for the capital murders for which they were instead serving prison terms, lives would have been spared. But the law has everywhere given judges or juries the power to impose either death or life imprisonment on one convicted of capital murder and in the vast majority of cases the latter punishment is selected. For instance, in California in 1963-1965, there were 531 persons convicted of murder, 225 of them (42.4 percent) for murder in the first degree, punishable by death, of whom 39 (17.3 percent) received a death sentence.[5] The rest were added to the prison population of capital murderers serving time for their crimes. Of the 16 known convicts who killed someone in California prisons during 1964 and 1965, none was in prison for capital murder.

Executing capital murderers in order to prevent them from killing in the future is not a feasible policy. Judges or juries are incapable of predicting the future conduct of a convicted murderer. It would be naive to imagine that courts could pick out from the mass of convicted murderers those who would commit a homicide in prison. Therefore, if the prevention of prison homicides by convicted murderers were the aim, all murderers would have to be sentenced to death and executed. No such policy would be tolerated by Americans.

Furthermore, of the 91 known killers in 1964-1965, only 15 were in prison for capital murder and 5 for noncapital murder, compared with 28 robbers, 11 thieves, and 10 burglars, the rest having been convicted of offenses distributed over eleven classes. We have already noted that 9 were in prison for capital crimes other than murder. Of the 91 killers, 58 were imprisoned for crimes of violence against the person.

---

5. Irvin W. Ramseier, *Willful Homicide in California, 1963-65* (Sacramento: Bureau of Criminal Statistics, 1967), p. 46.

A similar study, covering the years 1964 and 1965, was done in Canada on the basis of reports from all its penal institutions accepting prisoners with sentences of two or more years for felonies.[6] Two homicides occurred during the period studied. In 1964 a guard was killed by an 18-year-old prisoner who was serving a sentence of twelve years for violent robbery. The following year a 27-year-old prisoner, who was serving time for armed robbery, killed a fellow inmate.[7] Data for previous years were unavailable except for officers killed. During 1945-1963, three guards were killed. "One was killed in 1948 by a robber, one in 1961 by an unknown offender, and, finally, one in 1963 by fellow officers when in a panic they blindly fired into a cell where the victim was held hostage by two inmates convicted of robbery."[8]

The two most elaborate studies of prison homicide hitherto made are based on 1973 data and grew out of a research project supported by a federal grant.[9] Although they use the same data, the authors of the reports do not exploit them in the same manner. One concerned with the limited question of the conduct of capital murderers sentenced to prison would find in neither report information permitting a conclusive judgment. The Wolfson report does, however, pay some attention to the deterrent power of the death penalty and will therefore be examined more closely.

The data were gathered from 148 state and 24 federal prisons for male felons. No homicides occurred in 117 of these institutions and in 3 others, 1 excusable and 3 justifiable homicides were committed by prison guards, who shot 3 inmates trying to escape, and a fellow officer accidentally. The

6. Dogan D. Akman, "Homicides and Assaults in Canadian Prisons," in Thorsten Sellin, ed., *Capital Punishment,* pp. 160-168.

7. *Ibid.,* p. 163.

8. *Ibid.,* p. 166.

9. Sawyer F. Sylvester, John H. Reed, and David O. Nelson, *Prison Homicide* (New York: Spectrum Publications, 1977); Wendy Phillips Wolfson, "The Patterns of Prison Homicide," unpublished dissertation, University of Pennsylvania, 1978.

events in which convicts were the assailants occurred in 52
prisons and involved 124 victims, of whom 53 were killed by
single assailants, 35 by a total of 99 attackers, and 36 by persons unknown. Thus the number of known killers was 152. if
the unknown assailants were single or multiple in the proportions shown by those known, one would have to add about 64
unknown to the 152 known offenders, making a total of 216.
Information about the background, traits, and history of the
killers pertains to the 152 known offenders who constitute a
very large sample of the total. Of these, 47 were serving terms
for willful homicide, i.e., first- and second-degree murder
and non-negligent manslaughter, and 80 for attempted
homicide, aggravated assault, rape, or armed robbery; 15
were in prison for burglary, breaking and entering, or arson,
and 9 for drug offenses, leaving 1 whose offense was not
reported. Altogether, then, 83.5 percent of the killers were
serving time for crimes against the person. What we do not
learn from the report is the number and location of the killers
who were in prison for capital murder, but data communicated to the author by Dr Wolfson (June 22, 1979) show
that 19 of the offenders were serving sentences for first-
degree urder, 5 for second-degree murder, and 11 had life
sentences for murder — all in death-penalty states, except a
first-degree murderer in West Virginia and 3 lifers in New
Jersey, both abolitionist states.

Seven of the killings were the work of nine assailants who
were known to have committed a total of ten prison
homicides prior to 1973. They were all convicted of murder
and given sentences of at least ten years to run concurrently
with their present sentences.[10]

Of the 152 detected assailants, 107 were indicted, 57 of
them for murder and 8 for lesser offenses, leaving the charges
against the rest unclear. Only 87 were actually prosecuted and

10. Wolfson, *op. cit.*, p. 104.

61 of them convicted;[11] 47 were convicted of murder or manslaughter, for which none was sentenced to death; 12 were sentenced to life and 12 to 20 or more years; the rest received sentences about evenly divided between those with a minimum of 10 years or a maximum of 90 years. In almost all cases the sentences were to run concurrently with their present sentences.[12]

The overwhelming majority of the homicides occurred in prisons in death-penalty states — 117 in 26 of the 42 jurisdictions. Only 7 occurred in 4 of the abolition states. It is evident that the threat of capital punishment did not deter the assailants. Some of them were in prison for a crime for which they could have been sentenced to death, but no court could have foreseen that by sentencing them to imprisonment, it provided them with the opportunity to kill again.

Murderers on Parole

In the United States, convicts whose death sentences have been commuted or who have been sentenced to life imprisonment for murder may regain their freedom by being paroled after spending a decade or two in prison. Some are deprived of this opportunity, because they die a natural or violent death while in the institution. Some may be serving time in states that have laws barring the release of first-degree murderers or lifers, but even there the exercise of executive clemency may remove the barrier in individual cases. There is no need to discuss here the various aspects of the parole process when murderers are involved because we are concerned only with how such parolees behave once they have been set free. Do they, indeed, abuse their freedom and are they especially likely to prove a menace to the lives of their fellow citizens? It is fear of that menace that makes some people

---

11. *Ibid.,* Table 38.
12. *Ibid.,* p. 124.

favor capital punishment as a sure means of preventing a murderer from killing again after his return to freedom in the community. As we shall see, paroled murderers do sometimes repeat their crime, but a look at some facts will show that among parolees who commit homicides, they rank very low.

In 1969, 1970, 1972, and 1973, a total 6835 male convicts serving sentences for willful homicide were paroled from our state institutions. During the three years following the release of each of these four cohorts, 310 (4.5 percent) were returned to prison because they had violated parole regulations by committing a crime (21, or .31 percent, had committed willful homicide). The nature of that crime can be seen from Table 7.1. Of these violators, 21 (8.1 percent), had committed a willful homicide again, but we do not know who among them had been paroled from sentences for capital murder imposed in death-penalty states. It is safe to assume that most of them had been serving sentences for second-degree murder or voluntary manslaughter not punishable by death. Over half of the homicide recidivists had committed a crime of violence against the person, chiefly aggravated assault and armed robbery.

That parolees from sentences for willful homicide are not the ones most likely to kill someone while they are on parole can be seen from Table 7.2, in which we note that of the 58,265 convicts paroled during 1969, 1970, and 1972, the number violating their parole during the triennia following these years was 184, or 3.2 per thousand parolees. It is evident that those paroled from sentences for armed robbery, aggravated assault, and forcible rape, for instance, proved to be more homicidal than those who had been serving time for willful homicide, and that the burglars ran a close second to the latter.

---

11. *Ibid.,* Table 38.
12. *Ibid.,* p. 124.

Table 7.1: Crimes Committed by Male Willful Homicide Convicts During Three Years Following Their Release on Parole from State Institutions in 1969, 1970, 1972, and 1973, Respectively

Number paroled — 6835. Of these, 310 were returned to prison for new crimes of

Willful homicide	21
Armed robbery	66
Unarmed robbery	9
Aggravated assault	51
Forcible rape	9
Other sex crimes	6
Total	162
Burglary	35
Theft	17
Vehicle theft	7
Forgery, fraud, larceny by check	8
Violation, drug laws	11
Violation, alcohol laws	2
Other offences	68
Total	148

SOURCE: U.S. Department of Justice. *Sourcebook of Criminal Justice Statistics, 1975-78* (Washington, DC: U.S. Government Printing Office, 1976-79): 1975, Table 6.57; 1976, Table 6.115; 1977, Table 6.97; 1978, Table 6.79.

Interesting as these data are, they do not permit us to assess the conduct of first-degree or capital murderers who have been released on parole. They are concealed within the broad class of willful homicides, most of which are not punishable by death. What we need to know is whether capital murderers pose such threat to the lives of their fellow citizens that they

Table 7.2: Willful Homicides Committed by Male Convicts During Three Years Following Their Parole from State Institutions in 1969, 1970 and 1972, Respectively

Offence for Which Convict was Serving Time When Paroled	Number Paroled	Number Committing Willful Homicide	Rate Per 1,000 Parolees
Willful homicide	4,674	17	3.6
Negligent manslaughter	738	1	1.4
Armed robbery	6,806	42	6.2
Unarmed robbery	2,173	5	2.3
Aggravated assault	3,108	15	4.8
Forcible rape	1,262	5	4.0
Other sex offences	1,417	1	.7
Burglary	16,818	54	3.2
Theft, larceny	5,474	8	1.5
Vehicle theft	2,700	5	1.8
Forgery, fraud, larceny by check	5,148	12	2.3
Other fraud	469	4	8.5
Violation, narcotic laws	3,708	3	.8
Violation, alcohol laws	163	1	6.1
All others	3,607	11	3.1
Total	58,265	184	3.2

SOURCE: See Table 7.1.

should never be paroled. That information is not readily available, but the few studies referred to in the following paragraphs will suggest an answer.

During the 37 years ending May 1, 1969, a total of 607 lifers were released on parole from state correctional institutions in Pennsylvania. Because they had committed a new crime, 30 were returned to prison, but "only one repeated the crime of first-degree murder, which was committed during the holdup of a tavern." For this crime he was sentenced to death and executed. We do not know how many of these parolees had been in prison for first-degree murder, but nearly all had probably been, because of 249 lifers released on parole in 1954-1963, all but 3 had been in prison for that crime.[13]

In California, 342 male prisoners serving terms for first-degree murder were paroled during 1945-1954. By the middle of 1956, 11 had been returned to prison on convictions of misdemeanors, and of 9 others, 2 had new sentences for robbery, 2 for lewd acts with children, 1 for a narcotics offense, 1 for abortion, 1 for sex perversion, 1 for assault to murder, and, finally 1 for second-degree murder. None had committed a capital murder.[14]

In Michigan, an abolitionist state, all first-degree murderers receive life sentences. Between 1937 and 1952, paroles were granted to 68 who had served an average time of 22.5 years. Only 2 violated parole by committing a new crime: 1 was sentenced for burglary and the other for "indecent liberties."[15]

From January 1959 through November 1972, 268 first-degree murderers were paroled in Michigan after serving an average of 25 years. Only 1 was convicted of an offense while on parole. Late in 1970 after 2 years in freedom, he was found guilty of "failure to present a weapon for safety inspection." After 30 days in jail he was returned to prison as a

---

13. Commonwealth of Pennsylvania, Board of Probation and Parole, *Report on Lifers Released on Parole as of May 1, 1969* (Harrisburg, 1969); Commonwealth of Pennsylvania, Department of Justice, Bureau of Correction, *Time Served by Commuted Lifers...1954 to 1963* (Harrisburg, January 29, 1964). In order to be parolable in Pennsylvania, an offender sentenced to life imprisonment must have his sentence commuted by the Board of Pardons to a given number of years.

14. *Report of the Subcommittee of the Judiciary Committee on Capital Punishment Pertaining to the Problem of the Death Penalty and its Administration in California* (Assembly Interim Committee Reports 1955-1957, vol. 20, no. 3; Sacramento, 1957), p. 12.

15. Arthur Lewis Wood, "The Alternative to the Death Penalty," *The Annals,* vol. 284, November 1952, p. 71.

violator and again paroled early in 1972.[16]

From July 1930 to the end of 1961, there were 63 first-degree murderers released on parole from state prisons in New York. Of these, 61 had originally been sentenced to death; 56 had no previous felony convictions. Their mean age was 51 years and they had spent an average of 23 years in confinement, none less than 9 years and 7 of them 31 years or longer. By the end of 1962, 3 had been declared parole violators, 1 had been convicted of burglary after a year and a half on parole, and the other 2 were returned to prison for technical violations. None committed a homicide.[17]

During 1945-1961, New York releases on parole included 514 prisoners serving terms for second-degree murder. At the time, their mean age was 46 years. Most of them, 81 percent, had no previous felony conviction. "Of the 17 convicted of felonies [while on parole], 2, or .4 percent of the 514, were convicted of murder, first degree. One of the two... had been paroled after spending 17 years... the other after spending 13 years in prison." Within a month of his release on parole, one of them killed two drinking companions. The other killed nobody but did participate in an armed holdup during which a life was lost. Both were executed.[18]

"From 1945 through 1965, a total of 273 former first-degree murderers have been paroled in Ohio. Of this number... 15 became parole violators [but] only 2 have been returned for the commission of new crimes." One committed

16. Jack Schwartz, *Analysis of All Sentences Served in Michigan Penal Institutions for First-Degree Murder and Ended by Governor's Commutation between January, 1959 and November, 1972* (Lansing, Michigan: Lansing Community College, March 1973; mimeo.

17. State of New York, *Thirty-fourth Annual Report of the Division of Parole of the Executive Department for the Year January 1, 1963 to December 31, 1963* (Legislative Doc. 1964, no. 107), pp. 54-56.

18. *Ibid.*, pp. 56-58, 63. This material is also the subject of an article by John M. Stanton, "Murderers on Parole," *Crime and Delinquency*, vol. 15, January 1969, pp. 149-155.

armed robbery and the other an assault with intent to rob.[19]

Of ninety-two convicted murderers released on parole in Massachusetts, 1957-1966, five had been serving terms for murder in the first degree and eighty seven for second-degree murder. Eighteen of them were returned to prison as parole violators: eight for technical violations and eight who had been arrested for some offense but not brought to trial. Two had been convicted of a new crime: one of murder and one of assault with a deadly weapon.[20]

A recent study of murderers in Georgia, whose paroles were terminated "in the three-year period between 1973 and 1976 [sic]" either by discharge or by revocation due to the parolees' technical violation of a regulation or because they had committed a crime, revealed that of 58 whites, 1 had committed murder, 2 robbery, 1 a sex offense, 3 burglary, and 2 theft — 9 altogether, or 15.5 percent of the terminations. Of the 106 blacks, 32 (30.2 percent), were returned to prison because 7 had committed murder, 15 assault, 3 robbery, 1 sex offense, 2 burglary, 3 theft, and 1 forgery. Unfortunately, the authors do not indicate who among the parolees had been paroled from sentences for capital murder, nor do they mention the kind of homicide the parolees committed while on parole. It appears that when they speak of murder, they actually mean willful homicide. We are not told the number of parolees under supervision during the period studied and cannot, therefore, relate the number of parole violators to the population at risk.[21]

---

19. Ohio Adult Parole Authority, *A Summary of Parole Performance of First-Degree Murderers in Ihio for the Calendar Year 1965 and for the Period 1945-1965* (Columbus, June 1966).

20. Lygere Panagopoulos and Carroll T. Miller, *An Analysis of Recidivism Among Convicted Murderers* (Boston: Massachusetts Department of Correction, February 1970, publication 5097).

21. Alfred B. Heilbrun, Jr., Lynn C. Heilbrun, and Kim L. Heilbrun, "Impulsive and Premeditated Homicide: an Analysis of Subsequent Parole Risk of the Murderer." *Journal of Criminal Law and Criminology,* vol. 69, Spring 1978, pp. 110, 113.

The evidence presented shows that in general capital murderers rarely commit a homicide while on parole. One reason is that they constitute a select group. During 1930-1961, when 63 first-degree murderers were paroled in New York State, 327 went to the electric chair in Sing Sing prison and another sizable group (176 in June 1956) was retained in prison. In abolition states that group would be large, because attrition would occur only by death, pardon, or parole. Yet we have noted that prison homicides are not usually committed by prisoners serving sentences for capital murder and that such persons, whether in prison or on parole, pose no special threat to the safety of their fellowmen. In any case, capital punishment would not be a practical means of countering the threat.

Chapter 8

A MATTER OF RATES

When a capital murder is committed, the true retributionist's wish is that the law of talion be applied to the offender without fail. He is not primarily concerned with the frequency of murders in the community at a given time or over the years, but with the persons who committed these crimes — the murderers. Whether murders increase or decrease, he would regard retribution as achieved when all guilty of capital murder, be they few or many, have been executed, even if this were not the most useful way to protect society.[1] Were he interested in assessing the degree to which this goal is reached, he could do so by determining the number of persons who during a specified period of time, such as a year, committed capital murder and the number of such persons executed, which would permit the computation of an execu-tion rate demonstrating the relative success of capital retribu-tion. However, a true execution rate, unassailable by critics, can never be established, because the number of capital murderers can only be conjectured for reasons already given in an earlier chapter. Therefore, the only primary execution rates that can be produced must be based on the overt or visi-

---

1. "If it were shown that no punishment is more deterrent than a trivial fine, capital punishment for murder would remain just, even if not useful." Ernest van den Haag, "In Defense of the Death Penalty: a Legal-Practical-Moral Analysis," *Criminal Law Bulletin*, vol. 14, 1978, p. 67.

ble population at risk, i.e., persons suspected (arrested), prosecuted, or convicted of murder and preferably, of course, persons so processed for capital murder. Knowing the sex, age, race, and perhaps other specific attributes of such persons, secondary or special rates, which take these characteristics into account, would show whether or not capital retribution is applied in a selective or discriminatory manner.

Unlike the retributionist, who should be concerned only with execution rates, the researcher, who wants to know if the use of the death penalty is an effective means of restraining or deterring homicidal impulses of people living in states where the law threatens or punishes murderers with death, needs to construct murder, i.e., victim and murderer, rates, especially the latter, since it is on the minds of potential murderers that the fear of the death penalty is assumed to exercise a deterrent force. To construct such rates, the researcher must decide (1) what capital murders are and relate the number of *victims* of such events to the *population at risk* and (2) who capital murderers are and relate the number of such *murderers* to the population *capable of committing capital murder*. These relationships are commonly expressed in the form of rates per 1000, 10,000 or 100,000 of the appropriate population. Such rates can then be compared with execution rates, permitting inferences respecting the efficacy of executions in reducing the rates of murders or murderers.

It is noteworthy that students of general deterrence concerned with the function of capital punishment in that connection have depended on rates of victims and not on rates of murderers. Their researches on the deterrent effects of the death penalty have often been judged inconclusive and based on inappropriate data. In his brief of 1974 in support of the death penalty, the Solicitor General of the United States noted that "all of the available studies have evaluated the effect of the death penalty on the overall murder rate rather than on the rate of *capital murders*, and so the studies cannot exclude the possibility that the death penalty deters the commission of those murders to which it applies" (emphasis added).

This pertinent criticism was evidently forgotten by the author of the brief, because later in the document he suggests that "it could be argued that if the Court declared the death penalty unconstitutional and the murder rate increased, the increase would be evidence that a deterrent has been removed."[2] The murder rate to which he referred was, in fact, the "overall murder rate," which is actually the rate of "murder and non-negligent manslaughter" taken from the *Uniform Crime Reports* and which he had previously denounced as improper for use in testing the deterrent effects of capital punishment.

It is true that judgments of the effects of the threat or the infliction of the penalty of death on the frequency of murder have been made on the basis of very crude data, the rates of either (1) deaths due to willful homicides — murder and non-negligent manslaughters — known to the police, or (2) deaths due to homicide known to medical examiners or coroners who issue death certificates. Neither of these sources permit the segregation of capital murder victims. Some researchers have nevertheless based their judgments on the police data, others preferring the mortality data. All have tentatively assumed that within the totals of homicide victims known to these agencies, the quotas of capital murder victims remain constant.

Raymond Bye, who in 1917 first used homicide death rates in comparing the rates of abolitionist and retentionist states, noted that "there are two possible ways in which the extent of murder...might be measured. One is to take the actual number of cases that appear in the criminal courts, as shown in records of prosecutions or convictions." He decided

---

2. Robert H. Bork et al., *Brief for the United States as Amicus Curiae in the Case of Fowler* v. *North Carolina,* Supreme Court of the United States, October Term, 1974, pp. 36 and 37n.

against the use of such data because "they are not a perfectly accurate measure, for the number of murder cases prosecuted — much less the number of convictions — resting as it does upon the vigorous activity of the public attorneys or the efficiency of the courts, might not fairly represent the number of murders actually occurring in the community. . . . The other possibility is to take the homicide [i.e., the mortality] records of the various states," which "are probably more accurate and afford a basis for comparison by states. . . . But they are open to the objection that they include all cases of homicide, whereas to constitute a strictly fair test they should include only cases of deliberate murder, such as would constitute a murder in the first degree in a court of law, since it is only to that offense that the penalty of death applies. . . . At best," the homicide "figures can be little more than a rough approximation of the actual extent of murder technically punishable by death." He would have ignored them except for one consideration. "If the crime of murder in the sense above defined is sufficiently frequent to constitute as real a menace as those who favor the death penalty imply it is, and if the fear of death is as effective a deterrent in the case of this crime as these persons declare, it should make an appreciable difference between the homicide rates of those states which have capital punishment and those which have not."[3]

The assumption of a constant ratio of capital murders was questioned by Edwin Sutherland, because "there is no possibility of knowing whether this ratio is constant. Consequently, the ordinary practice of drawing conclusions regarding changes in murder rates from the changes in homicide

---

3. Raymond T. Bye, *Capital Punishment in the United States* (Philadelphia: The Committee on Philanthropic Labor of Philadelphia Yearly Meeting of Friends, 1918), pp. 41-42, passim. Clifford Kirkpatrick, in *Capital Punishment* (Philadelphia: The Committee on Philanthropic Labor of Philadelphia Yearly Meeting of Friends, 1925), also compared homicide death rates of contiguous states. It is regrettable that in the past writings of students of deterrence, including my own, these authors have not been given due credit for their innovation.

rates is logically invalid. But," he added, "it is the only method that can be used, since we have no other statistics available."[4] If this were true, there could be, of course, no justification at all for using such "logically invalid" data for the purpose mentioned.

My own view of this matter at the time was stated in a report to the Royal Commission on Capital Punishment in 1951, in which, like Bye 33 years earlier, I compared homicide death rates of contiguous abolitionist and retentionist states over a period of 29 years. Considering the impossibility of making an accurate count of *capital* murders and murderers,

> the student is compelled to search for statistical data, which may be assumed to reflect, even though they do not accurately, i.e., completely, portray the incidence of capital murder or murderers. If he is fortunate, he may find data on murders known to the investigating authorities (the police in Anglo-Saxon countries, the examining magistrates in others). The criminal statistician today tends to believe that these data can be used as an index to murder rates. If he is not quite so fortunate he will have to use data on deaths due to homicide. These are now available in most countries. Although they generally group all homicides together, studies comparing these death rates with rates of murder known to the police lead to the belief that they are reasonably good indicators of changes and trends in murder. One might assume that data on persons sentenced to death drawn from judicial criminal statistics would be a good indicator of the number of murderers, but strong reservations must be made in this connection, especially for countries with mandatory sentences. Data on persons sentenced for murder in general, however, or even on those charged with murder, probably have index

---

4. Edwin H. Sutherland, "Murder and the Death Penalty," *Journal of Criminal Law and Criminology,* vol. 15, 1925, p. 522. Both Bye and Sutherland, as well as Kirkpatrick, wrote before the establishment of the Uniform Crime Reporting System.

value, and even such sentences combined with sentences for voluntary manslaughter. Where such data are available, then, the studies needed to answer the...question[5]

of whether the annual number of executions for murder have any demonstrable relationship to the number of such crimes committed or to the number of persons committing murder, "are feasible." The implication of this statement is that if it were possible to construct rates of capital murder, they would parallel the rates of homicide deaths. This is a debatable assumption, as seen from the opinion of the Solicitor General already quoted, but researchers have generally adopted it, nevertheless, after many apologies and reservations.

A decade ago, Hugo Bedau stated that "capitally punishable homicide is probably a fairly constant fraction of the total volume of homicide, irrespective of how homicide itself is measured (by judicial, police or vital statistics),"[6] but later he concluded that the assumption "that homicides as measured by vital statistics are in a generally constant ratio to criminal homicides...is effectively unmeasurable because the concept of a criminal homicide is the concept of a homicide...which *deserves* to be criminally prosecuted."[7]

Gibbs and Erickson observed that "the relation between first degree murder rates and the other types of homicide rates remains unknown." They deplored "that so much research on the death penalty has not considered the appropriate kinds of crime rate, that is, for capital offenses *only*," and that they had "not found one instance where deterrence investigators have used a more relevant measure...such as the one based on the number of homicides

5. Royal Commission on Capital Punishment, *Minutes of Evidence,* Thirtieth Day, Thursday, 1st February, 1951; Witness: Professor Thorsten Sellin, p. 648.
6. Hugo Adam Bedau, ed., *Capital Punishment* (Garden City, NY: Doubleday, 1967), p. 73.
7. Hugo Adam Bedau, "Deterrence and the Death Penalty: a Reconsideration," *Journal of Criminal Law, Criminology and Police Science,* vol. 61, 1970, p. 545.

initially identified by the police as 'capital.' "[8] These are, of course, laudable goals which, for reasons already noted in an earlier chapter, are unreachable. Regrettably, rates of murder and capital murder will be based on less than complete and perfect data, a problem common to all research in the social sciences.

In spite of the implied promise of their titles, victimization surveys can be ruled out as a source of the data needed. Since the President's Commission on Law Enforcement and the Administration of Justice commissioned the first national survey ever done, covering the years 1965-1966, several other surveys have been undertaken by the Bureau of the Census.[9] These surveys are being hailed for providing a better basis for generalizations about the extent and trend of serious crimes, but as presently constructed they tell us nothing about criminal homicides, because they are based on interviews with living victims of crime. The part of the surveys concerned with crimes against households focuses on such crimes against property as burglary, household larceny, and motor vehicle thefts, and fails to ascertain if any member of the household was killed during the period surveyed. Were that done, we would have data on homicides for possible comparison with other national data on such events.

Since all murder rates are victim rates, and since the victims that can be counted will only be a sample — though probably very large — of an unknowable quantity, and that their classification as victims of murder can, in most cases, be done only after their assailants have been caught and the legal requisites for their prosecution and guilt have been established, is it indeed possible to find that firm basis for inferences,

8. Jack P. Gibbs and Maynard L. Erickson, "Capital Punishment and the Deterrent Doctrine," in Hugo Adam Bedau and Chester M. Pierce, eds., *Capital Punishment in the United States* (New York: AMS Press, 1976), pp. 306-307.

9. See, for instance, U.S. Department of Justice, National Criminal Justice Information and Statistics Service, National Crime Survey Report, *Criminal Victimization in the United States* (Washington, DC: U.S. Government Printing Office, December 1976).

which critics demand before accepting any conclusions regarding the effects of the death penalty on murder and murderer rates?

If it is decided that willful homicides known to the police or deaths due to homicide cannot be used for indices of murder, one possible solution might be to take the sum of (1) the victims of *unsolved* gangland murders and felony murders, which are by definition capital offenses, and (2) the victims in cases "cleared" by the prosecution or conviction of defendants in murder cases. Using murder cases instead of cases of capital murder so "cleared" can be defended as reasonable in view of the plea bargaining and other practices which, as justice is administered, blur the line separating capital from other murders. This does not rule out the possibility of paying special attention to first-degree murder prosecutions or convictions and subsequent executions.

Having decided which victims should be counted and having assembled data about them covering a given period of time — a year, for instance — in a given area, such as a state, murder rates can be computed. Since any living human being can be a murder victim it has become customary to compute such rates on the basis of the total population, in the hope that the effect of prosecutions, convictions, or executions of murderers will be reflected in changes in these rates over time. These rates are very crude, however, because they are based on an assumption that all segments of the population run the same risk of being murdered. That is not true. Just as miners, lumberjacks, and high-rise steelworkers run a greater risk of becoming victims of accidents than do college professors, so do members of some segments of the population run a greater risk of being murdered than others. Therefore, special rates are needed to measure the differential effect of the death penalty on population segments. Investigations of known murder victims can establish, accurately or with reasonable certainty, their sex, age, race, occupation, location of residence, and so on, and rates can be computed based on the population possessing these attributes, singly or in conjunction. For instance, has the prosecution, conviction, or execution of murderers of police officers any effect on the victim rate of police officers? Or do the convictions or executions of murderers of blacks or females have any noticeable effect on the victim rates of these population segments?

Parenthetically, leaving murder aside for the moment, the need for special rates is conspicuously demonstrated when we consider rape statistics. In the *Uniform Crime Reports* we find rape, i.e., rape victim rates, given per 100,000 population. This is not only a crude rate but a wrong rate, because it is based on the tacit assumption that all humans can be rape victims. It is true that occasionally males are raped — in prisons, for instance — but, as a rule, only females are raped and therefore a crude rape rate should be based on the female population at risk. Conversely, a crude rapist rate should be based on the capable male population. A long time ago, some states computed birth rates on a total population basis until they discovered that only women of child-bearing age could give birth to children.

Returning to murder, a different problem faces the researcher who wishes to compute rates of murderers. Here, too, the first step is to decide who are "murderers." Since they cannot be easily isolated from other offenders arrested for willful homicide, we are practically compelled to equate their number with the number of defendants indicted, prosecuted, or convicted of murder — possibly of capital murder, although for reasons already stated defendants in murder cases would probably serve our needs adequately.

Suppose it were decided to count as murderers only those convicted of that crime and that we have, let us say, annual data on their number and characteristics. To compute rates we now need a population base different from that used for murder rates, because though any human can become a murder victim, not everyone is a potential capital murderer. The population of persons capable of committing capital murder is restricted. It excludes, for instance, persons below a specified age — fifteen, let us say — in a given jurisdiction[10] and may, in fact, be limited in some jurisdictions — Rhode Island, before 1973, for instance — to the population of lifers confined in penal institutions. Therefore, instead of the now commonly used total population base for a crude murderer rate, this rate should be based on the population of *potential* murderers in the area — state or city — studied. The size of that population would presumably be recorded in the decennial censuses and in estimates made during intercensal years.

The crudity of even this revised rate is obvious. The census counts people living in the area on a given day, but the number of potential murderers in the area during a year, for instance, is much larger. Take a metropolitan city such as Philadelphia. There is a daily influx of people with jobs in the city but residing in surrounding communities, not counting tourists, shoppers, and other transients who are nonresidents. At any given time, they substantially increase the number of potential murderers in the area — and should they commit a crime, it is charged to the *resident* population when conventional rates are computed. This problem has led Professor Gibbs to speculate on what rates would afford more trenchant conclusions on the amount and trend of crime in an area than does a "conventional" rate which though "absolutely reliable...would not be satisfactory for deterrence research." The conventional rate to which he refers is the crude rate based on total population. Since his proposals are valid for all crimes, murder will be chosen to illustrate the six "unconventional" rates he defines:

(1) *crude de facto rate* based on the number of all persons spending any time, long or short, in the area during, let us say, a year

---

10. About 27 percent of the U.S. population was under fifteen years of age in 1950 and 28 percent in 1970.

(2) *refined de facto rate* based on the total time (e.g., hours or days) which everybody spent in the area during a year

(3) rate of murder by area residents (*residential rate*) based on the number of residents in the area for any period of time during a year

(4) *refined rate of (3)* based on total time (days or hours) spent in the area by residents during a year

(5) rate of murder by residents born in and always residing in the area (*nativity rate*) based on the number, at mid-year, of residents in and born in the area

(6) *refined rate of (5)* based on the total time spent by such residents in the area during a year

Theoretically speaking, Professor Gibbs thought that "with a view to the putative cognitive assumptions of the deterrence doctrine and the opportunity factor, investigators should use a residential or nativity crime rate (preferably the refined versions)," but he concluded that "they cannot do so," because no matter how desirable such rates might be, they could not be computed by anybody who did not possess "astronomical resources."[11]

What all this means is that we are left with the conventional crude rates. As for rates of murderers, we must keep in mind that the risk of becoming a murderer also varies with the sex, age, race, and other possible attributes of a person. Special rates based on such population components are needed, especially since their relative proportions in the total population often change substantially over time, producing unanticipated changes in the conventional murder rate. These general and special rates can, like murder rates, be used to test the efficiency of the death penalty in protecting life.

The upshot of this analysis is that the hope of ever unearthing absolutely perfect data for the construction of unassailable murder or murderer rates is a mirage, and that

---

11. Jack P. Gibbs, *Crime, Punishment and Deterrence* (New York: Elsevier, 1975), pp. 41-42.

both those who support and those who oppose the death penalty for some reason or other, as well as impartial students, will always be — and are — compelled to fall back on rates which represent reality only approximately.

In my own attempts to measure the deterrent force of capital punishment I have looked for its effects over time on the rates of death due to homicide in death-penalty states and have compared these rates with those of neighboring abolition states on the assumption that states in such clusters would be reasonably alike in the makeup of their populations and their socioeconomic characteristics. I have preferred to use the homicide death rates rather than the willful homicide rates for several reasons. First, nearly all states issued them annually long before the FBI began to publish its rates in 1933 in the *Uniform Crime Reports* (UCR). Second, the mortality rates were based on death certificates submitted by responsible authorities in all parts of a state, while the crime rates in the UCR were, until quite recent times, based only on the population of the cities participating in the voluntary reporting program. The number of these cities was 740 in 1930, 1078 in 1945, and 2781 in 1957. Before World War II half of their populations lived in cities with over 250,000 inhabitants. Since homicide rates have always been highest in the largest cities, this meant that the size of the willful homicide rate of a state depended on the proportion of large-city populations in the total population of the cities reporting. Finally, the rates given in the UCR were useless before 1958, being based on the population of the reporting area as given in the latest decennial census. This resulted in a spurious rise in crime rates during intercensal years, because the crimes known to the police in 1949, for instance, were still being charged to the 1940 population. The effect of this practice was especially noticeable in rapidly growing states whose people, seeing crime rates dropping in each census year, must have been amazed at the beneficial influence of the census.

Beginning with 1958, the annual rates of willful homicide

reported in the UCR have been based on the estimated population at mid-year in the reporting area.[12] As the number of police agencies reporting to the FBI increased, the validity of its crime rates improved. Progress toward the development of more reliable homicide rates was accelerated by the passage of the Omnibus Crime Control and Safe Streets Act in 1968, which enabled the Law Enforcement Assistance Administration (LEAA) to assist states financially in setting up agencies capable of furnishing the FBI with complete statewide data required for its annual *Uniform Crime Report*. By 1973, 22 states had such services, and by 1978 the number of states that can be said to have been admitted to the registration area for police statistics had risen to 43. Within a few years, when all the states have joined, a truly national rate of willful homicide will be available, as a national homicide death rate has been since 1933.

Despite the flaws in the police data mentioned, researchers on deterrence who use them consider them superior to rates based on mortality data. Ehrlich, whose research, published in 1975, created a stir by his assertion that, based on aggregate "murder rates," his "empirical analysis suggests that on the average the tradeoff between the execution of an offender and the lives of potential victims it might have saved was of the order of magnitude of 1 for 8 for the period 1933-1967 in the United States,"[13] explained that

> With respect to...the murder rate, the figures I have used are based on the Federal Bureau of Investigation's revised estimates of annual total murders and nonnegligent manslaughters. For the purposes of the empirical investigation, the FBI data are conceptually superior to the homicide

---

12. This reform was made in response to my criticism of the old practice given in an interview reported in a widely circulated monthly magazine. See Robert Wallace, "Crime in the United States," *Life,* vol. 43, September 9, 1957, p. 49.
13. Isaac Ehrlich, "The Deterrent Effect of Capital Punishment: a Question of Life and Death," *American Economic Review,* vol. 65, June 1975, p. 398.

series published in the *Vital Statistics of the United States*, because the FBI category is defined to include any willful felonious homicides. Law enforcement officials, not health officials, bear the responsibility and undergo training for distinguishing willful felonious homicides from other homicides.

Furthermore, "the homicide data of the FBI reflect the agency's unique opportunity to incorporate in its estimates whatever homicide data have been collected by health officials."[14] By contrast, he found the mortality data inferior because "by definition the homicide data of the *Vital Statistics* explicitly include justifiable homicides and are likely to include some negligent manslaughters as well." Also, "the homicide figures tabulated for the *Vital Statistics* are never revised after the last cutoff date for data collection for a given year. In addition, information on death certificates, on which the *Vital Statistics* figures are based, sometimes may reflect classification of deaths only by medical cause rather than by external cause (such as accident or homicide), especially in those instances when death from homicidal assaults occurs later than the time of assault."[15] Yet Ehrlich adds that "tests which I have been conducting with independent bodies of data...indicate, nevertheless, that the effects of the deterrence variables — including the conditional probability of execution — on the homicide rate as reported by the *Vital Statistics* are qualitatively the same as those found in my time series investigation."[16] Thus, it would appear that the systematic differences in the bases of the two series of rates are sufficiently constant to make either series useful as indices of murder.

Tables 8.1 and 8.2 may tell us whether or not we can trust

---

14. Isaac Ehrlich, "Deterrence: Evidence and Inference," *Yale Law Journal*, vol. 85, 1975, p. 212.
15. *Ibid.*
16. *Ibid.*, p. 213.

that assumption. In Table 8.1, willful homicide and homicide death rates are compared over a period of 40 years in Michigan, Ohio, and Indiana. Inspection of the table reveals that except for the first 5 years in Michigan and Ohio, the willful homicide (or crime) rates were always higher than (or identical to) the death rates, until the last decade when this trend was reversed. With rare exceptions, the two rates rose or fell together from one 5-year period to the next.

Table 8.1: Willful Homicide Rates (WH) and Homicide Death Rates (H): Michigan, Ohio, and Indiana, 1935-1974 (Mean Annual Rates Per 100,000 Population)

Quinquennia	Michigan		Ohio		Indiana	
	WH	H	WH	H	WH	H
1935-1939	2.9	3.9	5.7	5.9	5.1	4.5
1940-1944	3.7	3.2	4.8	4.3	3.7	3.0
1945-1949	4.5	3.5	5.6	4.8	5.4	3.8
1950-1954	4.3	3.8	4.1	3.8	4.4	3.7
1955-1959	3.8	3.0	3.8	3.4	3.9	3.0
1960-1964	3.6	3.6	3.2	3.2	3.7	3.2
1965-1969	6.2	6.6	5.0	5.1	4.2	4.7
1970-1974	11.0	11.3	7.6	7.8	6.3	6.4

SOURCE: *Uniform Crime Reports* and *Vital Statistics of the United States.*

In Table 8.2 a comparison is made between the two rates in randomly selected states and for the years 1967-1971 and 1972-1975, the 1976 death rates not being ready. Of the 24 states, 17 belonged to the registration area for police statistics, though none earlier than 1969 and most of them only since 1973 or 1974.

Table 8.2: Homicide Death Rates (H) and Willful Homicide Rates (WH) Compared, 1967-1975 (Mean Annual Rates Per 100,000 Population)

| States | Registration Area States | | | |
| | H Rates | | WH Rates | |
	1967-1971	1972-1975	1967-1971	1972-1975
Arizona	7.3	9.9	6.8	8.4
Arkansas	8.5	9.8	9.5	10.1
California	6.9	9.5	6.7	9.4
Delaware	7.6	9.0	7.1	7.6
Idaho	3.4	4.6	3.3	4.3
Illinois	8.9	9.0	8.6	10.4
Iowa	1.6	2.6	1.7	2.1
Kentucky	9.2	10.2	9.7	10.0
Maryland	8.4	11.5	9.4	11.6
Minnesota	2.1	2.8	2.0	2.8
Nebraska	2.7	3.8	2.6	3.8
New Mexico	7.8	12.0	8.0	11.8
Oregon	3.6	5.2	3.6	5.5
Tennessee	11.0	13.8	9.7	12.3
Virginia	8.7	11.1	7.6	9.5
West Virginia	5.1	5.8	5.7	6.3
Wisconsin	2.4	3.3	2.2	2.9
	Nonregistration Area States			
Colorado	5.6	7.2	5.5	7.4
Missouri	9.2	9.8	9.2	9.4
Montana	4.1	5.2	3.4	4.5
North Dakota	1.0	1.6	.7	1.1
South Dakota	2.5	3.7	2.9	2.7
Washington	4.0	5.0	3.5	4.8
Wyoming	4.4	5.2	6.4	5.5

SOURCES: *Uniform Crime Reports* and *Vital Statistics of the United States.*

The table shows that in only 8 of the 24 states were the H rates higher than the WH rates during both periods of years. The WH rates were higher than the H rates during both periods in Maryland, West Virginia, and Wyoming. The rates can be said to be identical during both periods in California, Colorado, Idaho, Minnesota, Missouri, Nebraska, New Mexico, and Oregon. In the rest of the states both rates rose from one period to the other, except in South Dakota and Wyoming where the H rate rose but the WH rate declined.

No matter how complete and accurate the periodic reports of homicide deaths and willful homicides are for a given jurisdiction and span of time, the decision on which series to use in deterrence studies is still a toss-up, since for most states of the union today, either series would seem equally acceptable — and equally useless in deterrence research since executions have ceased or become too rare to have any possible influence on the murder rate. Having opted for the homicide death rates, they will be the ones I shall rely on in the review of the experiments with the death penalty in the United States to which the last two chapters will be devoted.

Chapter 9

EXPERIMENTING WITH DEATH

It has been said that the nonexperimental research to which the study of the deterrent effect of capital punishment is necessarily limited almost certainly will be unable to meet the "extremely severe standards of proof" which legislators should require scientific evidence to meet before accepting it as a basis for public policy.[1] It is, of course, true that no researcher would be allowed to set up a controlled experiment that would prove the presence or absence of the deterrent effect of capital punishment, nor would public authorities be able to do it in democratic states, but legislators, courts, and pardon authorities do institute experiments. When a legislature, for instance, abolishes or introduces the death penalty for murder, it usually does so, at least in part, in the belief that this action will produce observable results. It does, in fact, engage in an experiment and this experiment can be studied to determine, for instance, its impact upon the murder rates of the state in question. Many American states have, indeed, embarked on such experiments, as did the Supreme Court of the United States, when it placed an em-

---

1. Alfred Blumstein, Jacqueline Cohen, and Daniel Nagin, eds., *Deterrence and Incapacitation: Estimating the Effects of Criminal Sanctions on Crime Rates* (Washington, DC: National Academy of Sciences, 1978), p. 63.

bargo or moratorium on executions in 1967, a prohibition which was to last for a decade.

The belief that capital punishment is both a sure means of safeguarding people's lives by the fear it engenders in the minds of potential murderers and a merited retributive penalty for those who wantonly kill someone found its expression in the capital laws of all American states until 1846, when Michigan abolished death for murder nine years after the state's admission to the union. The proviso that the act would not take effect before March 1847 was inconsequential as there had been no execution since September 4, 1830, under the territorial government, when Stephen G. Simmons was publicly hanged in Detroit for the murder of his wife.[2] The hanging caused public opinion to turn

> against such executions and this feeling was accentuated in 1838 by the hanging of a man by the name of Fitzpatrick at Sandwich, Ontario, directly across from Detroit. Fitzpatrick was declared guilty by the Canadian court on circumstantial evidence, but a few months after the execution...a man by the name of Sellers made a deathbed confession of the crime for which Fitzpatrick had been hanged.[3]

Michigan's abolition law was the end product of a movement of penal reform activated by a mixture of religious sentiments and concepts of human rights and of what proper public policy in a democratic state should be. It was a movement of relatively recent origin, nurtured by the philosophers of the Enlightenment, especially Rousseau. Its most famous spokesman was Cesare Beccaria, whose essay, *Dei delitti e delle pene* (*Of Crimes and Punishments*), published in Italy in

---

2. Louis H. Burbey, "History of Execution in What is Now the State of Michigan," *Michigan History Magazine,* vol. 22, 1938, pp. 443-457. The Northwest Ordinance, passed by Congress in 1787, applied to a vast area including the present states of Ohio, Indiana, Illinois, Michigan, and Wisconsin. In 1805, Michigan received a separate territorial government.

3. *Ibid.,* p. 452.

1764, called for the abolition of the death penalty and its replacement by a punishment that would be more effective as a deterrent in preventing crime.[4] This view won adherents in Europe, among whom Empress Catherine II of Russia, Grand Duke Leopold of Tuscany, and Emperor Joseph II of Austria were the most illustrious examples. Within five years of its publication, the essay had been twice issued in English in London and in 1773 an American edition appeared in New York. Its importance was quickly realized. In 1770, a young Boston lawyer, John Adams, respectfully quoted Beccaria when he addressed the jury in "defense of the British soldiers implicated in what became known as 'The Boston Massacre.' "[5] Thomas Jefferson shared or was converted to this view of the "unrightfulness and inefficacy of the punishment of crimes by death," but recognized that "the general idea of the country had not yet advanced to that point."[6] And in 1787, Benjamin Rush, prominent Philadelphia physi-

---

4. This was no novel demand. In various ages and states, it had led to the abolition of capital punishment. According to an ancient historian, Diodorus Siculus, Sabbacus, an Ethiopian king of Egypt in the eighth century, B.C., put no criminals to death, sending them, instead, in chains to labor on public works. During the Roman Republic, citizens of Rome condemned to die were allowed to go into exile. In Japan, the death penalty was abolished in the ninth century "as a concession to Buddhism" (G. B. Sansom, *Japan*, rev. ed., Tokyo: Tuttle, 1973; orig. published London, 1931, p. 215). Emperor Leo III (717-741 A.D.) of Byzantium substituted mutilation for death. This practice was mentioned by the philosopher Plethon (1355-1450) in a communication to Manuel Paleologus. "With us, Sire, there are men to be found, guilty of the gravest offenses, who are in most cases under sentence of death. Actually, this penalty, as things now stand, has fallen into desuetude; the judges condemn some of the offenders to mutilation and they dismiss a great number practically unpunished. Neither extreme seems to me to be right. Mutilation is barbarous...but it is also most injurious...that criminals should be left unpunished. A form of punishment which in my view is better...is that criminals should be set to work in chains" on public works (Ernest Barker, *Social and Political Thought in Byzantium,* Oxford: Clarendon Press, 1957, pp. 30-31, 204). In Russia, Empress Elizabeth (1741-1761) abolished capital punishment in her realm in 1744.
5. Marcello Maestro, *Cesare Beccaria and the Origin of Penal Reform* (Philadelphia: Temple University Press, 1973), p. 137.
6. *Ibid.,* p. 141, quoting from Jefferson's *Autobiography.*

cian, published *An Enquiry into the Effects of Public Punishments upon Criminals and upon Society* in which he wrote, "I have said nothing upon the manner of inflicting death as a punishment for crimes because I consider it as an improper punishment for any crime," and referred to the "Marquis of Beccaria's excellent treatise upon this subject." He repaired this omission in 1792 with the publication of an essay, *Considerations on the Injustice and Impolity of Punishing Murder by Death*, which clearly shows Beccaria's influence.

The greatest of the early American abolitionists, however, was Edward Livingston who, in his report in 1822 to the Louisiana legislature on his plan of a penal code and in the introduction to this Code of Crimes and Punishments in 1824, presented masterful analyses of why the death penalty should be abolished.[7] They provided powerful arguments to those who, in various states of the North before the Civil War, were spearheading a growing movement to abolish capital punishment, a movement which would succeed in Michigan, Rhode Island, and Wisconsin a decade or more after Livingston's death.[8]

Michigan

Michigan's pioneer law of 1846 substituted lifelong solitary

---

7. *The Complete Works of Edward Livingston on Criminal Jurisprudence,* 2 vol. (New York: National Prison Association, 1873), vol. 1, pp. 35-59, 190-224; partially reproduced in Philip English Mackey, "Edward Livingston on the Punishment of Death," *Tulane Law Review,* vol. 48, December 1973, pp. 25-42; Jerome Hall, "Edward Livingston and his Louisiana Penal Code," *American Bar Association Journal,* vol. 22, March 1936, pp. 191-196.

8. Philip English Mackey, "Edward Livingston and the Origins of the Movement to Abolish Capital Punishment in America," *Louisiana History,* vol. 16, Spring 1975, pp. 145-166; David Brion Davis, "The Movement to Abolish Capital Punishment in America, 1787-1861," *American Historical Review,* vol. 43, October 1957, pp. 23-46; Louis Filler, "Movements to Abolish the Death Penalty in the United States," *The Annals,* vol. 284, November 1952, pp. 124-136.

confinement at hard labor for hanging. Since then all attempts to restore the death penalty for murder have been defeated in the legislature or by popular referendum. The law had retained the death penalty for treason, a crime which no one could commit short of war between the state and its neighbors. This anomaly was finally removed in 1963, prompted by the hanging of a federal criminal at the Federal Detention Farm at Milan, Michigan, in 1938, much against the protest of state authorities.[9]

The effect of abolition on the murder rate of Michigan is problematical due to the absence of proper data before the present century. During 1847-1858, 30 prisoners were convicted of first-degree murder and admitted to the state prison — an average of 2.5 annually. Before the end of the twelve-year period, 1 of these was pardoned, 6 had died, and 1 had received a commutation of his sentence to nonsolitary hard labor for life. During the next nine years, 12 capital lifers were received, averaging 2.3 per year.[10] More useful data for testing the hypothesis that a demonstrable relationship exists between the size and the trend of the murder rate of a state and its use, disuse, or nonuse of the death penalty have been developed during the present century. They are the number of deaths due to homicide reported to health authorities and the more recent number of willful homicides known to the police agencies of a state, and they can be used to construct crude rates that take account of the changes in the size of the population on which the rates are based. But homicide rates are influenced by many factors over time, such as the rate of urbanization, changes in the age, race, and sex compositions of the population, economic and political changes, and the

---

9. Federal law provided that if a federal offender was convicted of a capital crime within a state having the death penalty he could be executed in a federal institution within the state, using the method provided by state law. See Burbey, *op. cit.,* pp. 456-457.

10. Marvin H. Bovee, *Reasons for Abolishing Capital Punishment* (Chicago, 1978), pp. 256, 260.

like. To isolate the influence of capital punishment would seem to be a hopeless task. One possible approach, described in Chapter 8, would be to compare the homicide rates of a state lacking the death penalty with the corresponding rates of neighbor states that use that punishment. In the case of Michigan, its rates could be compared with those of Ohio and Indiana, of which especially the former has been a frequent executioner.

In Table 9.1 the mean homicide death rates of the three states are given for five-year periods, 1920-1974, as well as the number of executions in Ohio and Indiana. Until the 1960s Michigan's rates were generally lower than Ohio's and most of the time lower than Indiana's, but all three states showed rapid increases after 1965, especially Michigan.

Table 9.1: Crude Homicide Death Rates: Michigan, Ohio, and Indiana, 1920-1974
(Mean Annual Rates Per 100,000 Population)

Quinquennia	Michigan	Ohio		Indiana	
		Rates	Number of Executions	Rates	Number of Executions
1920-1924	5.5	7.4	45	6.1	5
1925-1929	8.2	8.4	40	6.6	7
1930-1934	5.6	8.5	43	6.5	11
1935-1939	3.9	5.9	29	4.5	22
1940-1944	3.2	4.3	15	3.0	2
1945-1949	3.5	4.8	36	3.8	5
1950-1954	3.8	3.8	20	3.7	2
1955-1959	3.0	3.4	12	3.0	0
1960-1964	3.6	3.2	7	3.2	1
1965-1969	6.6	5.1	0	4.7	0
1970-1974	11.3	7.8	0	6.4	0

SOURCE: National Office of Vital Statistics, *Vital Statistics of the United States*; William J. Bowers, *Executions in America* (Lexington, Mass: D.C. Heath, 1974), appendix A.

NOTE: After 1949 homicides caused by police intervention and legal executions have been deducted before rates were computed.

Rhode Island

In Rhode Island, the abolition movement of the 1830s was illustrated by a report to the General Assembly in 1838. Its authors cited "the philosophy of Franklin, the philanthropy of a Rush and the research of a Livingston" and urged the abolition of capital punishment.[11] This recommendation was not approved, but the legislature did abolish the penalty for several crimes, reserving it for murder and arson, with life imprisonment as an alternative punishment for the latter crime.[12] Finally, in 1852, the death penalty was removed from the penal code and life imprisonment at labor substituted. Among the factors contributing to this decision was the widespread belief

> that the verdict in the famous Gordon murder trial of 1844 was a travesty of justice and that the bench had allowed racial prejudice to influence its decision. The Gordon brothers, two Irish immigrants, were charged with the murder of the industrialist Amasa Sprague, who had opposed the licensing of their tavern. When Sprague's mutilated body was discovered, the Gordons were immediately suspected and, though the evidence against them was flimsy and circumstantial, they were brought to trial. The court found John Gordon guilty and sentenced him to death, but it released his brother. Coming, as it did, so soon after the Dorr War, in which the opponents of reform had deliberately appealed to nativist, Protestant prejudices, the trial seemed to many to have been a mockery of justice. Though the reaction to Gordon's execution contributed eight years later to the abolition of capital punishment, the case left bitter memories in the Irish community.[13]

11. State of Rhode Island, in General Assembly, January 23, 1852, *Report of the Committee on Education in the Senate, on the Subject of Capital Punishment* (Providence, 1852), p. 41.
12. Edward Field, ed., *Rhode Island and Providence Plantations at the End of the Century: a History*, 3 vol. (Boston: Mason Publishing Co., 1902), vol. 3, p. 444.
13. Peter J. Coleman, *The Transformation of Rhode Island, 1790-1860* (Providence: Brown University Press, 1963), p. 243.

The death penalty was reintroduced in 1882 for murder committed by a prisoner serving a life sentence. In 1973, this specification was broadened "to include any prisoner committed to confinement to the adult correctional institutions of the state or the state reformatory for women." No one has been executed in Rhode Island for this crime.

How did abolition affect the homicide rates of the state? The only available data for early years consist of the annual number of convictions for murder. During the seven decades between 1838 and 1907, these numbers were 3, 8, 9, 6, 10, 10, and 11, respectively, a nearly fourfold increase, but between 1840 and 1910 the resident population of the state increased even faster, from 109,000 to 543,000.[14] When we compare the homicide death rates of the state with the rates of the border states of Massachusetts and Connecticut, which used the death penalty, we find that during 1920-1974 Rhode Island and Massachusetts show almost identical rates, slightly exceeded by Connecticut.

Wisconsin

The third of the early abolition states was Wisconsin, which achieved territorial status in 1838. Statutes adopted the following year provided the death penalty for murder, and this provision was included in the first compilation of laws in 1849, following the admission of the state into the union the previous year. The penalty seems to have been used two or three times before one John McCaffary was hanged on August 21, 1851, at Kenosha for the murder of his wife. This public spectacle, attended by between two and three thousand people was to be the last execution in the state.[15]

---

14. The statistics of convictions were furnished by the office of the Governor of Rhode Island to Professor M. Liepmann. See his *Die Todesstrafe. Ein Gutachten* (Berlin: Guttentag, 1912), p. 64.

15. C. Cropley, "The Case of John McCaffary," *Wisconsin Magazine of History*, vol. 35, 1952, pp. 281ff.

Table 9.2: Crude Homicide Death Rates: Rhode Island, Massachusetts, and Connecticut, 1920-1974 (Mean Annual Rates Per 100,000 Population)

Quinquennia	Rhode Island	Massachusetts		Connecticut	
		Rates	Number of Executions	Rates	Number of Executions
1920-1924	2.5	2.6	3	3.3	4
1925-1929	2.5	2.1	16	2.8	4
1930-1934	1.9	2.1	7	2.6	2
1935-1939	1.6	1.6	11	2.0	3
1940-1944	1.1	1.3	6	2.0	5
1945-1949	1.5	1.4	3	1.7	5
1950-1954	1.2	1.1	0	1.6	0
1955-1959	1.2	1.0	0	1.5	5
1960-1964	1.2	1.6	0	1.7	1
1965-1969	2.4	2.7	0	2.5	0
1970-1974	3.3	4.0	0	3.4	0

SOURCES and NOTE: See Table 9.1.

Efforts to abolish the death plenalty had been made several times during the territorial period and a bill to that effect passed in the Assembly in 1847 but was defeated in the Senate. The trial of William B. Radcliffe in 1852 in Milwaukee climaxed the movement. "Radcliffe admitted that he had killed a drinking companion and robbed him, but the confession was not admitted at the trial held before 1500 people in the opera house. The jury refused to convict on circumstantial evidence. . . The case added impetus to the movement against capital punishment because it showed the reluctance of a jury to convict when the penalty was death."[16] In

---

16. *The Milwaukee Journal,* May 12, 1851, quoted in Wisconsin Legislative Reference Library, *Information Bulletin,* vol. 210, March 1962, p. 2.

1853, a select committee of the Senate, chaired by Marvin H. Bovee, introduced an abolition bill which passed both houses and made life imprisonment the sole punishment for first-degree murder.[17] Since then sporadic attempts in recent decades to restore the penalty have all failed.

Wisconsin's murder rates have been low. During the four quinquennia, 1890-1909, the mean rates, per 100,000 population, of persons convicted of murder were 3.8, 2.7, 2.0 and 2.4, respectively.[18] If we compare the homicide death rates of the state with those of the border states of Minnesota and Iowa during 1920-1974, the similarity of the rates is striking, although Iowa was a death-penalty state. Minnesota abolished that punishment in 1911; judging from the subsequent decline of its rates abolitionists might, without justification, be tempted to attribute this trend to the change of punishment.

Iowa

With Wisconsin's law the abolition movement came to a halt. Other social issues were pressing for attention, and the Civil War and Reconstruction would be foci of thought and activity. During the rest of the century only four states would experiment with abolition, and the first of them was Iowa.

The land now occupied by that state was first opened for settlement in 1833 and by the time the 1840 census was taken, two years after the establishment of the territory of Iowa, the resident population numbered 43,000. The first hanging took place in Dubuque on June 20, 1834, after the solemn trial of Patrick O'Connor for the murder of George O'Keaf.[19] The territorial law of 1838 made murder punishable by death and

---

17. *Laws of 1853,* Chapter 103.
18. Based on data supplied by the Office of the Governor to Professor Liepmann. See his *op. cit.,* p. 63.
19. T. F. Hollowell, "Some Iowa Criminal History," *Bulletin of State Institutions,* vol. 24, April 1922, p. 132.

**Table 9.3: Crude Homicide Death Rates: Wisconsin,
Minnesota, and Iowa, 1920-1974
(Mean Annual Rates Per 100,000 Population)**

			Iowa	
Quinquennia	Wisconsin	Minnesota	Rates	Number of Executions
1920-1924	1.9	3.4	2.4	6
1925-1929	2.4	2.7	2.5	2
1930-1934	2.8	3.3	2.8	1
1935-1939	1.7	1.9	1.8	7
1940-1944	1.3	1.6	1.3	3
1945-1949	1.2	1.5	1.5	4
1050-1954	1.2	1.3	1.3	1
1955-1959	1.1	1.1	1.1	0
1960-1964	1.5	1.2	1.3	2(4)*
1965-1969	2.1	1.9	1.6	0
1970-1974	3.0	2.5	2.1	0

SOURCES and NOTE: See Table 9.1.
*Number of prisoners received with death sentences from courts during quinquennium.

after the admission of the state into the union in 1846, a new penal code limited this penalty to first-degree murder and treason. The death penalty was abolished in 1872, reestablished in 1878, and again abolished in 1965. Until 1894, executions took place in the counties.

The abolition act of 1872 was one result of a budding movement after the Civil War to restrict the use of the death penalty in the young prairie states. A few years earlier, Marvin Bovee, untiring apostle of abolition, had prophesied that Iowa, Missouri, and Nebraska would very soon abandon capital punishment; only Iowa would do it. (He failed to mention Kansas, which became a de facto abolition state in 1872, but more on that later.) The repeal of the Iowa statute in 1878 may be understandable considering its timing. The nation was experiencing its worst economic depression. It had started with the panic of 1873, would not begin to ease up until late in 1878, and reached its climax the previous year with the great national railroad strike which bankrupted most railroads and spawned widespread violence. Crime was reported on the rise everywhere, and vagrancy increased alarmingly.[20] And yet other factors may well have been responsible for the repeal, since none of the other abolitionist states was tempted to take such action although plagued by the same social ills.

It is evident that Iowa has been a reluctant user of the death penalty. After the repeal, only two hangings seem to have occurred, one in 1887 in Floyd County and one the following year in Fayette County.[21] When executions were transferred to the state penitentiary in 1894, one man was hanged there that year and one in 1895, following which a decade would pass without executions. During the five quinquennia, 1900-1944, the mean annual numbers of persons convicted of murder were 12.4, 12.6, 18.6, 16.0, and 20.2.[22] There was one execution in 1906, one in 1910, and six in 1922-1924. Most executions occurred after 1921; their distribution has already been given in Table 9.3. After 1952 only two hangings took place, both in 1962, three years before the state again abolished this penalty.

The homicide death rates of Iowa, compared with those of its abolitionist neighbors, Minnesota and Wisconsin, have

20. Ellen Elizabeth Guillot, *Social Factors in Crime* (Philadelphia, 1943), pp. 106-111; Robert V. Bruce, *1877, Year of Violence* (Indianapolis: Bobbs-Merrill, 1959), Chapter 1; Philip Taft and Philip Ross, "American Labor Violence: Its Causes, Character, and Outcome," in Hugh Davis Graham and Ted Robert Gurr, eds., *Violence in America: Historical and Comparative Perspectives* (Washington, DC: National Commission on the Causes and Prevention of Violence, 1969), vol. 1, pp. 226-228.
21. Hollowell, *op. cit.,* p. 140.
22. *Biennial Reports of the Secretary of State Relating to Criminal Convictions, 1900-1908.* In 1908 the newly created State Board of Parole was entrusted with the publication of these reports.

been shown in Table 9.3. Its neighbor Nebraska, an equally reluctant death penalty state, had somewhat higher rates during 1920-1974, as seen in Table 9.4.

Table 9.4: Crude Homicide Death Rates: Nebraska (Mean Annual Rates Per 100,000 Population)

Quinquennia	Rates	Number of Executions
1920-1924	4.4	3
1925-1929	3.4	5
1930-1934	3.7	0
1935-1939	2.3	0
1940-1944	1.7	0
1945-1949	2.0	2
1950-1954	2.0	1
1955-1959	2.1	1
1960-1964	2.1	0 (1)*
1965-1969	2.6	0 (1)*
1970-1974	3.3	0

SOURCES and NOTE: See Table 9.1. The next and last execution was in 1959.

*Number of prisoners received with death sentences from courts during quinquennium.

Kansas

In 1872, eleven years after gaining statehood, Kansas passed a statute similar to the one that Maine had adopted in 1837. It provided that no person sentenced to death could be executed until a year had passed and then only if the governor of the state signed a death warrant. The effect was that no governor took such action before 1907; that year the legislature made life imprisonment the maximum punishment for murder until 1935, when the death penalty was restored. The state's Supreme Court declared it unconstitutional in January 1973. The first executions, three in number, took place in 1944, and the last of twelve subsequent hangings in 1965.

During the years 1920-1974, the homicide death rates of the state compare favorably with those of its neighbors, Missouri and Colorado. In spite of some fluctuations, the rates of all three states tended to decline until the 1960s. Execution figures for Missouri are lacking before 1930 becaue hangings took place in the counties until 1937, and figures for 1930-1936 exist only because in 1930 the Bureau of the Census began publishing them based on death certificates.

Table 9.5: Comparative Homicide Death Rates: Kansas, Colorado, and Missouri (Mean Annual Rates Per 100,000 Population)

Quinquennia	Kansas		Missouri		Colorado	
	Rate	Number of Executions	Rate	Number of Executions	Rate	Number of Executions
1920-1924	6.3	—	10.9	?	10.5	3
1925-1929	5.4	—	11.0	?	7.2	4
1930-1934	6.4	—	11.8	16	8.0	16
1935-1939	4.1	—	7.5	20	5.8	9
1940-1944	3.0	3	5.0	6	3.7	6
1945-1949	2.9	2	6.2	9	4.9	7
1950-1954	2.9	5	5.6	5	3.4	1
1955-1959	2.5	0	5.3	3	3.6	2
1960-1964	2.7	1	5.0	3	4.5	5
1965-1969	3.3	4	7.8	1	4.7	1
1970-1974	4.8	0	9.6	0	6.6	0

SOURCES and NOTE: See Table 9.1.

Maine

As already noted, Maine adopted a law in 1837 that practically abolished capital executions. The hanging of Joseph Sager in Augusta two years earlier had aroused great controversy and a year later a committee of the state senate, chaired by Tobias Purrington, recommended the abolition of capital punishment. The result was a compromise which gave the chief executive discretionary power to order the hanging of a murderer, but not until a year had elapsed since the death sentence was imposed. Until 1864, when the incumbent governor signed the death warrant of Francis Couillard, who had murdered the warden of the state prison, governors had come to regard the statute in question as manifesting the legislature's rejection of the death penalty.

The execution of Couillard revived the abolitionist movement. Early in 1869, Senator John L. Stevens introduced an order in the senate instructing the judiciary committee to report a bill abolishing capital punishment. From his published remarks on this occasion,[23] it appears that the governor either had or was going to order the hanging of Clifton Harris, a Negro and recent migrant, about whose case "there is deep mystery...that has not yet been unraveled." Harris was indeed hanged a month later and so were two men in 1875. The following year the legislature abolished the death penalty. It was reintroduced in 1883, but three hangings in 1885 were to be the last in Maine, because two years later it was again abolished — permanently.

The administration of capital justice in Maine is illustrated in Table 9.6, based upon reports of the state's attorney general. It shows that the mean annual number of homicide convictions rose gradually from 1860 on, reached a peak during the years that the death penalty was in force, and fell

---

23. *Remarks of John L. Stevens in the Senate of Maine February 11 and 12, 1869*...(Augusta, 1869).

thereafter. Meanwhile, the resident population of the state increased from 628,000 in 1860 to 694,000 in 1900.

Table 9.6: Persons Prosecuted, Convicted, and Executed for Homicide: Maine, 1890-1903
(Mean Annual Numbers)

Years	Prosecuted	Convicted	Executed
1860-1863	16.5	1.8	—
(1864-1869)	12.5	2.2	1
(1870-1875)	13.0	2.7	2
1876-1882	7.4	3.6	—
(1883-1886)	7.5	6.2	3
1889-1893*	5.8	3.6	—
1894-1898	7.8	4.6	—
1899-1903	6.6	3.6	—

SOURCE: *Ohio State Library Bulletin,* Vol. 1, 1906, pp. 7-8.
NOTE: Parentheses cover years when the death penalty was in use.
*Reports missing for 1887 and 1888.

One alleged reason for the elimination of the death penalty was the belief that juries were loathe to convict murderers when the law mandated death as the only punishment for their crimes, with the result that murder often went unpunished. The above table fails to furnish evidence of the validity of that belief. The percentage of homicide defendants convicted was, in fact, lowest during the last few years of de facto abolition — 10.6 percent. It rose to 19 percent when executions were resumed, to 49.2 percent during the abolition years 1876-1882, and, contrary to expectations, peaked to 83.3 percent during 1883-1886. For the years 1889-1903, the percentage was 60.4.

The homicide death rates of Maine compare favorably with the rates of other states in its region. Table 9.7 gives these rates for Maine and its two neighbor states that had the death penalty, New Hampshire and Massachusetts.

Table 9.7: Comparative Homicide Death Rates: Maine, New Hampshire, and Massachusetts, 1920-1974 (Mean Annual Rates Per 100,000 Population)

Quinquennia	Maine Rates	New Hampshire Rates	Number of Executions	Massachusetts Rates	Number of Executions
1920-1924	1.7	2.0	0	2.6	3
1925-1929	1.6	1.1	0	2.1	16
1930-1934	1.9	1.5	0	2.1	7
1935-1939	1.5	1.6	1	1.6	11
1940-1944	1.9	.8	0	1.3	6
1945-1949	1.4	.9	0	1.4	3
1950-1954	1.6	1.0	0	1.1	0
1955-1959	1.3	1.1	0	1.5	0
1960-1964	1.6	1.2	0	1.7	0
1965-1969	1.5	1.6	0	2.5	0
1970-1974	2.6	2.1	0	3.4	0

SOURCES and NOTE: See Table 9.1.

Colorado

The last state to experiment with abolition during the nineteenth century was Colorado. It did so early in 1897, but in

1901 the death penalty was restored. The lynchings of two blacks and a white man the previous year and mounting unrest and disturbances in the mining regions appear to have been the overt causes of the reaction. During the five years prior to abolition, the mean annual number of convictions for murder in the state was 16.3. The corresponding numbers for the abolition years and the subsequent five-year period was 18 and 19.[24] It would have been useful to compare the state's homicide death rates with those of its neighbors before, during, and after the abolition years; but this is impossible since Colordao was not admitted to the registration area for vital statistics until 1906 and its neighbor states even later, between 1910 and 1929.

We have looked at the successful attempts in a few states to remove the death penalty from the statute books during the nineteenth century. The effects of this legislation on the homicide rates of the states involved have been examined but the results of the evaluation will be left until we have paid attention to developments during the present century.

---

24. Liepmann, *op. cit.,* p. 69, citing data from Ohio State Library, *Monthly Bulletin,* vol. 50, no. 10, p. 14.

Chapter 10

THE TWENTIETH CENTURY

During the first decade of the present century fruitless efforts were made to secure the abolition of capital punishment in this or that American jurisdiction. The social reformers of the progressive era were concerned with other matters. It was during the second decade that the abolitionists would score their greatest successes. No fewer than eight states removed the death penalty for murder, beginning with Minnesota in 1911, followed by Washington in 1913, Oregon in 1914, Tennessee, South Dakota, and North Dakota in 1915, Arizona in 1916, and Missouri in 1917. Before the end of the decade, the legislators of Tennessee, Arizona, and Washington, seemingly appalled by their rashness, would hurriedly reinstate the death penalty, as would Oregon in 1920.[1] South Dakota would return to capital punishment in 1939, but after executing a man in 1947 would again abolish the penalty in 1977. Oregon became abolitionist again in 1964, and North Dakota, which had retained the death penalty for first-degree murder committed by a prisoner serving life for such murder

---

1. Except for a brief quotation from a Nashville newspaper, noting the abolition of the death penalty for murder in Tennessee, there is no mention of these experiments in any of the articles or among the news items published in the prestigious *Journal of the American Institute of Criminal Law and Criminology,* which began publication in 1910.

but had never imposed it, removed the exception in 1975. Minnesota never lost its aversion to the taking of the life of a criminal.

When the Supreme Court of California declared, early in 1972, that the infliction of capital punishment violated the state constitution's prohibition of the infliction of cruel and unusual punishments and the Supreme Court of the United States a few months later, in the Furman case, decided that the death penalty was unconstititional, the goal of the abolitionists seemed to have been reached. Prior to these events, Alaska and Hawaii had removed the death penalty in 1957 and Iowa and West Virginia in 1965. Delaware had experimented with abolition during 1958-1961. The expectations of the abolitionists were premature, however. The Furman decision had loopholes. The Court had found that as presently practiced the use of the death penalty was unconstitutional, but left open the possibility that it would approve its use under certain conditions. Nearly all the states that had the death penalty prior to the Furman decision reenacted death penalty statutes, most of which were found defective by the Court in 1976. In New Jersey (1972), Massachusetts (1975), Maryland and New Mexico (1976), and Kansas and the District of Columbia (1977), death penalty statutes were held to be unconstitutional. At the end of 1977, 15 states and the District of Columbia were abolitionist. At that time there were 443 prisoners on death row in 22 states.

What prompted the states to engage in these experiments and why the ambivalence reflected in the restoration of a penalty once discarded? A careful study might reveal the motive forces producing these acts, but few of them have been subjected to analysis. Equally important, of course, is the determination of the effect they had on the trends of murder, when potential perpetrators of that crime were suddenly freed from or again faced the danger of capital punishment. These aspects of the problem will be examined in the pages that follow.

Washington

The first legislature of the territory of Washington, meeting in 1854, provided the death penalty for first-degree murder. No attempt to change the law seems to have been made before 1897 when an abolition bill was passed by the House but rejected by the Senate. Several later legislatures debated the issue until March 1913, when the opponents of capital punishment finally won the argument — but not for long. The very next legislature debated the restoration of the penalty and in March 1919 this was accomplished. Fear of a crime wave following World War I seems to have been one reason, but a more forceful one may have been the murder in the State House, in 1917, of the state industrial insurance commissioner by a man who "boasted that the state could do nothing to him but board him for the rest of his life."[2]

The best measure available of the effect of this legislation is the homicide death rate of the state. During the five years preceding abolition, the mean annual rate was 6.5 per 100,000 population, and that rate was also recorded for 1913. The year after abolition the rate rose to 10.0 and then declined during the next four years to 8.9, 5.5, 5.5, and 4.2, respectively. The year the death penalty was reintroduced showed a rate of 7.5 the following five-year period had a mean annual rate of 5.4. During 1908-1912 6 men were executed, and 5 during 1920-1924. Rates for 1920-1974 are given in Table 10.1 and compared with the rates of Oregon and Idaho.

Oregon

In its Article I, Sec. 15, the 1859 Constitution of Oregon provided that "laws for the punishment of crime shall be founded on the principles of reformation, and not of vindic-

---

2. Norman S. Hayner and John R. Cranor, "The Death Penalty in Washington State," *The Annals,* vol. 284, November 1952, p. 101. He served his life sentence in full when he died in the penitentiary of natural causes in 1921.

tive justice." This would seem to make the death penalty un-constitutional, if the reform of the offender was the aim, but in another section the framers ordered mandatory capital punishment for murder in the first degree, and since then courts have found these seemingly contradictory provisions compatible.[3]

Attempts to abolish the death penalty were defeated until 1914, when the following constitutional amendment, strongly supported by the governor, was submitted to the voters in November — "The death penalty shall not be inflicted on any person under the laws of Oregon. The maximum punish-ment that may be inflicted shall be life imprisonment." Though no one expected a favorable vote, the amendment was adopted by a majority of 157.

A special session of the legislature was called by the gover-nor in 1920 and he addressed it as follows:

Since the adjournment of the regular session in 1919 a wave of crime has swept over the country. Oregon has suffered from this criminal blight, and during the past few months the commission of a number of cold-blooded and fiendish homicides has aroused our public to a demand for greater and more certain prosecution.... . [Therefore] the people of the state should be given an opportunity to pass upon the ques-tion of the restoration of capital punishment and that there should be no unnecessary delay in bringing this question before the electorate.[4]

This was promptly done. A constitutional amendment restor-ing the death penalty for first-degree murder but leaving to the jury the power to substitute life imprisonment for it in a given case was adopted by a substantial majority of the voters

---

3. *State* v. *Finch,* 1909, cited by Hugo Adam Bedau, "Capital Punishment in Oregon, 1903-64," *Oregon Law Review,* vol. 45, December 1965, p. 37.
4. Quoted by Robert H. Dann, "Capital Punishment in Oregon," *The Annals,* Vol. 284, November 1952, p. 111.

in the November election. On November 3, 1964, 44 years later, Oregon voters again removed the death penalty by a vote of 455,654 to 302,105.

Washington's experiment with abolition had already ended in 1919 and Oregon's would not begin until 1965, but it is nevertheless interesting to inspect the homicide death rates of these states compared with those of their neighbor, Idaho, which prescribed death for murder during the 1920-1974 period but used the punishment very rarely. From Table 10.1 it is evident that both the trends and the sizes of the homicide death rates of the three states were remarkably similar.

Table 10.1: Crude Homicide Death Rates: Washington, Oregon, and Idaho, 1920-1974
(Mean Annual Rates per 100,000 Population)

| Quinquennia | Washington* | | Oregon | | Idaho | |
	Rates	Number of Executions**	Rates	Number of Executions	Rates	Number of Executions
1920-1924	5.4	5	5.0	7	4.1	1
1925-1929	4.7	6	4.0	8	4.0	1
1930-1934	5.4	10	4.3	1	4.0	0
1935-1939	3.8	13	3.4	1	3.9	0
1940-1944	3.0	8	3.2	6	2.3	0
1945-1949	3.3	7	3.3	6	3.2	0
1950-1954	2.7	4	2.6	4	2.5	2
1955-1959	2.6	2	2.4	0	2.4	1
1960-1964	2.8	2	2.8	1(5)	2.4	0(1)
1965-1969	3.4	0(4)	3.4	—	2.9	0
1970-1974	4.6	0(3)	4.7	—	4.3	0

SOURCE and NOTE: See Table 9.1

*Numbers in parentheses represent number of prisoners received from courts with death sentences during quinquennium.
**Number of persons executed during quinquennium.

Missouri

In April 1917, the Missouri legislature adopted a statute that made it unlawful "to take human life as a punishment for crime." The event evoked the usual reponses from the public. Some favored, others opposed the move and a concerted effort to restore the penalty took form headed by law enforcement authorities who were aroused by the killing of several peace officers by criminals. In one instance, a prisoner in jail at Lamar killed the sheriff and his son during an attempt to escape. He was tried, convicted, and sentenced to life imprisonment, but a mob broke into the jail and lynched him early in June 1919. The following month, at a special session of the legislature, capital punishment was reenacted. Previously, the governor had "been in communication with the governors of eleven states in which capital punishment had been abolished, and they had been asked if crime had increased. 'None said that it had increased, and eight declared that it had not.' "[5] During the five years prior to abolition, the mean annual homicide death rate of the state was 9.3, rising to 10.7 during 1917-1919, and continuing the rise after the restoration to 10.9 during 1920-1924, hardly a reassuring development for the advocates of capital punishment. Since then, the rates of the state have remained consistently higher during the quinquennia of 1920-1974 than those of its neighbor states of Illinois, Iowa, and Kansas, but lower than those of Arkansas. The sizes and trends of the rates of Missouri, Kansas, and Iowa have already been shown in Tables 9.3 and 9.5. Therefore, only the rates of Illinois and Arkansas will be given in Table 10.2.

Tennessee

The abolitionist sentiments and arguments voiced by Rush and Livingston were echoed by Aaron V. Brown who, as

5. Ellen Elizabeth Guillot, "Abolition and Restoration of the Death Penalty in Missouri," *The Annals,* vol. 284, November 1952, p. 108.

Table 10.2: Crude Homicide Death Rates: Illinois and Arkansas, 1920-1974
(Mean Annual Rates per 100,000 Population)

Quinquennia	Illinois*		Arkansas**	
	Rates	Number of Executions	Rates	Number of Executions
1920-1924	9.0	33	—	16
1925-1929	10.2	35	16.0	19
1930-1934	10.0	34	15.7	20
1935-1939	6.2	28	11.2	33
1940-1944	4.4	13	9.1	20
1945-1949	5.2	5	8.1	18
1950-1954	4.3	8	6.7	11
1955-1959	4.3	1	6.6	7
1960-1964	4.5	2(13)	7.0	9(8)
1965-1969	7.2	0(28)	7.2	0(10)
1970-1974	9.3	0(9)	9.7	0(7)

SOURCE and NOTE: See Table 9.1. Numbers in parentheses are the number of prisoners with death dentences received from the courts each quinquennium.

*For executions in Illinois prior to 1928, see State of Illinois, *Eleventh Annual Report of Department of Public Welfare, July 1, 1927 to June 30, 1928* (Springfield, II, 1929), p. 455.

**Arkansas entered registration area for vital statistics in 1927.

chairman of the judiciary committee of the stat senate, in 1831 authored a lengthy report advocating the removal of capital punishment — to no avail. As governor of the state in 1845, he informed the legislature that he would "with the greatest pleasure" commute all death sentences in cases "authorized by law and justified by their circumstances."[6]

6. Fred Travis, "Crusade against Death," *Chattanooga Times,* January 5, 1958, p. 16.

Later sporadic efforts to change the law were equally unsuccessful until 1915, when a wealthy merchant of Memphis, Duke C. Bowers, led a "crusade against the death penalty extended to what is reported to have been lavish entertainment of legislators in Nashville."[7] A bill retaining the death penalty for rape but abolishing it for murder passed both houses and became law without the governor's signature, but the very next legislature restored the penalty for murder early in 1917. According to Governor A. A. Taylor, in a communication to Governor Harry L. Davis of Ohio, capital offenses increased during the period of abolition and *especially rape*, although this was the crime for which the death penalty had been retained.[8] Unfortunately, Tennessee did not enter the registration area for vital statistics until 1918, making the computation of acceptable homicide death rates possible. In Table 10.3, comparative rates are given for 1920-1974 for Tennessee and its northern neighbor, Kentucky. For the rates of its western neighbor, Arkansas, see Table 10.2.

Delaware

In April 1958, a well-directed abolition campaign ended with the removal by the legislature of the death penalty for five crimes, including first-degree murder. Two weeks earlier the *Wilmington Morning News*, in an editorial, had given its support to the impending proposal but warned that "the innovation will still be on trial. One particularly revolting crime during the next few years or a wave of the sort of crimes to which the death penalty formerly applied could bring an outcry for the restoration of capital punishment."[9] The warning was prophetic. On June 10, 1961, "an eighty-nine-year-old

---

7. *Ibid.*
8. Harry L. Davis, "Death by Law," *Outlook,* July 26, 1922.
9. Quoted by Herbert L. Cobin, "Abolition and Restoration of the Death Penalty in Delaware," in Hugo A. Bedau, ed., *The Death Penalty in America,* rev. ed. (Garden City, NY: Anchor, 1967), p. 364.

Table 10.3: Crude Homicide Death Rates: Tennessee and Kentucky, 1920-1974
(Mean Annual Rates per 100,000 Population)

	Tennessee		Kentucky	
Quinquennia	Rates	Number of Executions	Rates	Number of Executions
1920-1924	16.6	18	13.0	12
1925-1929	17.2	9	16.2	25
1930-1934	20.1	16	18.7	18
1935-1939	18.3	31	16.4	34
1940-1944	12.4	20	11.3	19
1945-1949	11.5	18	10.3	15
1950-1954	8.2	1	7.8	8
1955-1959	7.9	7	6.5	8
1960-1964	7.4	1(7)	6.8	1(10)
1965-1969	9.6	0(1)	7.9	0(12)
1970-1974	13.0	0(13)	10.0	0(8)

SOURCE and NOTE: See Table 9.1. Numbers in parentheses are the number of prisoners received from the courts with death sentences during each quinquennium.

woman was badly beaten and stabbed to death in Georgetown, Delaware, the rural county seat in the southern part of the state. The victim was a well-known, well-liked and highly respected church-going widow."[10] On June 12, the mayor of Georgetown, who was a member of the state senate, introduced a bill to restore the death penalty, and two days later it was passed. The bill was poorly drafted, however, and before amendments were acted upon by the House, the abolitionists had gathered enough strength to permit them to ex-

Ibid., p. 366.

pect a defeat of the bills had an event not occurred which dashed their hopes. "On October 13, on a farm seven miles from the small town of Laurel, Delaware, Kermit West, a twenty-five-year-old Negro killed an elderly couple with a shotgun."[11] Within six weeks both houses restored capital punishment for first-degree murder and promptly overrode the governor's veto.

The murders just described apparently triggered the reaction which Cobin believed to be provoked by discordant race relations. Certainly an important factor, suggestive for further study, was

> the impact of these two crimes involving the killing of three elderly white persons, two of them women, by young Negroes at the very time when racial tension was high for several reasons: the desegregation movement at the school systems; a strong demand from Negroes for anti-discrimination and civil rights laws... 'action' and 'sit-in' groups seeking to desegregate restaurants in lower Delaware and along Route 40 to Washington, D.C.[12]

The behavior of the legislature is a classical example of the victory of passion over reason. Abolition had not led to an increase of murder. During the two fiscal years preceding abolition 45 persons had been committed to correctional institutions on charges of murder. During the *four* years, 1958-1962, 55 persons were so committed and during the next four years 71 persons. Of these 171 individuals, 17 had life sentences for second-degree murder and 7 for first-degree murder: 2 were sentenced to death but not executed.[13] The last execution in Delaware occurred in 1946, when a Negro male was hanged in Sussex County for murder.

---

11. *Ibid.,* pp. 368-369.
12. *Ibid.,* p. 372.
13. Glenn W. Sammuelson, "Why was Capital Punishment Restored in Delaware?" *Journal of Criminal Law, Criminology and Police Science,* vol. 60, June 1969, pp. 148-151.

During the five years before the repeal of the death penalty the state's annual homicide death rate averaged 5.4 per 100,000 population. The corresponding rate during 1958-1961 was 4.4 and during the five years after the penalty was restored, it returned again to 5.4. When we compare the rates of the state during the years 1920-1974 with the rates of Maryland and New Jersey, we note the similarity of the rates of Delaware and Maryland, but although the New Jersey rates are generally lower, they show the same trend. In January 1972, the death penalty law of New Jersey was declared unconstitutional by the state's Supreme Court and on September 1, 1979, a new criminal code went into effect, containing no death penalty for murder.

Table 10.4: Crude Homicide Death Rates: Delaware, Maryland, and New Jersey, 1920-1974
(Mean Annual Rates per 100,000 Population)

Quinquennia	Delaware* Rates	Number of Executions**	Maryland Rates	Number of Executions	New Jersey Rates	Number of Executions
1920-1924	6.3		6.8		4.8	22
1925-1929	6.9		7.5	11	4.6	12
1930-1934	10.4	2	8.4	6	4.9	24
1935-1939	7.1	6	7.4	10	3.1	16
1940-1944	5.5	2	7.7	26	2.3	6
1945-1949	6.4	2	7.9	19	2.9	8
1950-1954	5.6	0	5.9	2	2.5	8
1955-1959	4.7	0	5.1	4	2.2	9
1960-1964	4.8	0	5.7	1(15)	2.6	3(13)
1965-1969	7.4	0(2)	8.5	0(8)	4.2	0(18)
1970-1974	8.4	0(2)	9.9	0(6)	6.3	0(3)

SOURCE and NOTE: See Table 9.1. Numbers in parentheses show number of prisoners with death sentences received from courts during a quinquennium.
*Delaware executions take place in the counties. Beginning in 1930, the Bureau of the Census counted them on the basis of death certificates supplied to the Bureau.

Table 10.5: Crude Homicide Death Rates: North Dakota, South Dakota, Montana, and Wyoming, 1920-1974
(Mean Annual Rates per 100,000 Population)

Quinquennia	North Dakota Rates	South Dakota Rates	South Dakota Number of Executions	Montana Rates	Montana Number of Executions	Wyoming Rates	Wyoming Number of Executions
1920-1924	2.1*			7.0		15.0**	1
1925-1929	1.5	***		8.8		10.6	0
1930-1934	1.9	2.1	0	8.0	1	9.2	3
1935-1939	1.9	1.4	0	5.2	4	4.2	1
1940-1944	1.3	1.4	0	3.6	1	4.8	2
1945-1949	.9	1.7	1	3.7	0	4.8	1
1950-1954	.7	1.4	0	3.4	0	2.8	0
1955-1959	.8	1.5	0	3.4	0	3.6	0
1960-1964	1.3	2.1	0	3.3	0	4.2	0(1)
1965-1969	.8	2.3	0(1)	3.1	0	4.9	1(1)
1970-1974	1.6	2.9	0	5.2	0	4.1	0(4)

SOURCE and NOTE: See Table 9.1. Numbers in parentheses are number of prisoners with death sentences received from courts.

*1924 rate; state admitted to registration area that year.

**State admitted to registration area in 1922.

***South Dakota admitted in 1930.

Minnesota and the Dakotas

In 1911 Minnesota became the first state during the present century to abolish capital punishment. During 1898-1911 (data for 1906-1907 missing) the mean annual number of persons prosecuted for murder was 17 and the number convicted 7.9. During the first five abolition years the corresponding figures were 11.2 and 7.6, which seems to indicate that it was easier to secure convictions for capital murder after abolition.[14] Minnesota was admitted to the registration area for vital statistics in 1910. For that year and for 1911, its homicide death rates were 3.3 and 3.9, respectively, followed by rates of 2.8, 3.0, 4.5, and 3.3 after abolition. The homicide death rates of the state for the 1920-1974 period have already been given and compared with the rates of Wisconsin and Iowa in Table 9.3. Its western neighbors, North and South Dakota, had abolished the death penalty for murder in 1915, the latter reinstituting it in 1939. In Table 10.5 their rates are compared with those of the death penalty states of Montana, west of North Dakota, and of Wyoming, west of South Dakota.

Arizona

Between December 8, 1916 and December 8, 1918, Arizona was an abolition state. Governor Thomas E. Campbell, in a personal communication to Governor Harry L. Davis of Ohio, reported that during the two years before abolition 41 murderers were convicted in his state, that 46 were convicted during the abolition years, and 45 the following two years.[15]

In Table 10.6, homicide death rates of Arizona are given for 1926 (year admitted to registration area) through 1974. Rates beginning 1920 for California and 1930 for New Mexico are also given for comparison.

---

14. Bye, *op. cit.,* p. 51.
15. Davis, *op. cit.*

Table 10.6: Crude Homicide Death Rates: Arizona, California, and New Mexico, 1920-1974 (Mean Annual Rates per 100,000 Population)

Quinquennia	Arizona		California		New Mexico	
	Rates	Number of Executions**	Rates	Number of Executions	Rates	Number of Executions
1920-1924		9	9.1	33		
1925-1929	14.0	7	7.2	45		
1930-1934	12.8	7	7.3	50	13.5	2
1935-1939	10.7	10	5.9	57	9.2	0
1940-1944	6.8	6	4.6	35	5.7	0
1945-1949	6.4	2	5.2	48	7.0	2
1950-1954	6.7	6	4.0	39	5.4	2
1955-1959	7.1	4	3.6	35	5.0	1
1960-1964	6.1	0(16)	4.1	29(93)	6.2	1(1)
1965-1969	6.4	0(10)	6.0	1(90)	6.6	0(3)
1970-1974	9.4	0(2)	9.0	0(67)	11.3	9(7)

SOURCE and NOTE: See Table 9.1. Numbers in parentheses are number of prisoners with death sentences received from courts during quinquennium.

West Virginia

West Virginia abolished the death penalty in 1965. Its homicide death rates are compared with those of Virginia in Table 10.7, but might also be compared with the rates of Kentucky given in Table 10.3 and those of Ohio in Table 9.1.

We have now looked at the states of the union that have temporarily or permanently abandoned the death penalty for murder, and we have observed the effect of such actions on

Table 10.7: Crude Homicide Death Rates: West Virginia and Virginia, 1920-1974
(Mean Annual Rates per 100,000 Population)

Quinquennia	West Virginia		Virginia	
	Rates	Number of Executions	Rates	Number of Executions
1920-1924			11.3	
1925-1929	12.3		10.7	
1930-1934	13.3	10	13.7	8
1935-1939	9.2	10	12.7	20
1940-1944	6.3	2	9.6	13
1945-1949	6.9	9	9.4	22
1950-1954	5.3	5	8.3	15
1955-1959	4.3	4	7.5	8
1960-1964	3.1	0	6.6	6(10)
1965-1969	4.3	—	7.9	0(3)
1970-1974	5.6	—	10.2	0(10)

SOURCE and NOTE: See Table 9.1. Numbers in parentheses are number of prisoners with death sentences received from the courts during quinquennium.

the incidence of that crime in the abolitionist states compared with the experience of their retentionist neighbors. The purpose of these comparisons has been to uncover evidence of the power of the death penalty to deter people from committing murder. If the absence or the discarding of this penalty were to add to the perils threatening life, those advocating the retention or adoption and adequate use of capital punishment would have a valid argument in its favor.

The study of the comparative rates in the tables of this and the preceding chapter leads to the conclusion that they yield no support for the belief in the deterrent power of the death

penalty. Within each cluster of states, abolitionist and retentionist states yield rates remarkably similar in both size and
trend and generally favor the abolitionist states, at least when
they have practiced abolition for long periods of time.

This conclusion has not gone unchallenged. First, can we
use the homicide death rates as an index to murder? Would
not rates based on the number of willful homicides known to
the police be superior? The pros and cons have been discussed in Chapter 8, where the use of the death rates has been explained and defended. Neither rate can provide more than
approximate measurements. This is well understood by all
who use these rates in deterrence research and implicitly
assume that the quota of capital murder hidden in the rates
constitutes a constant proportion of the recorded homicides.
The correctness of this assumption is difficult to prove and is
generally taken on faith.

Second, in measuring the effect of capital punishment on
the murder rates of abolitionist and retentionist states, the
criteria governing the designation of a state as retentionist
become important. In our tables a state has been so classified
if its statutes provided the death penalty for murder. This is
said to be misleading, because such a state may not *use* the
penalty and is therefore actually de facto abolitionist. True —
but how often should the death penalty be applied in a state
to allow us to classify it as a death-penalty or a retentionist
state for comparative purposes? In Table 9.7 the rates of
Maine, New Hampshire, and Massachusetts have been compared, Maine being the abolitionist state in the cluster. New
Hampshire executed a man in 1939, the first — and the last —
execution in 21 years. If a state has had no execution in 40
years, it should probably be called de facto abolitionist.
Before the death penalty was made inoperative by the U.S.
Supreme Court in 1967, no one had been executed in
Massachusetts or South Dakota since 1947, in Delaware since
1946, or in Montana since 1943. In most of the clusters of
states examined, however, the death penalty was exacted

more or less consistently by the retentionist components, but I leave to readers, who have looked at the tables, to decide for themselves what years or periods a "death-penalty state" deserved that appellation, since researchers have reached no agreement on the definition.

We know that most murders are committed by males in the 18-35 age group, that blacks commit relatively more murders than do whites, that people over 60 rarely kill anybody, that the proportion of children in the population may change over time due to changes in the birth rate, that urbanization brings with it an increase in crimes of violence, such as felony murders, and that changes in the economic well-being of social classes influence the homicide rate. The dimensions of these factors should be taken into account in comparative research. To use a crude example, the rise in the crude homicide rate over a period of years may be due chiefly to an increase in the proportion of young and young adult males in the population rather than to the absence or reduced use of capital punishment. In our comparisons of homicide death rates these socioeconomic and demographic variables and their criminogenic roles have been assumed to be roughly identical in their distribution and function in contiguous abolitionist and retentionist states. The remarkable similarity of the amounts and trends of the rates in the clusters suggests that the assumption is not completely gratuitous.

Tests of the validity of the assumption have been attempted. Baldus and Cole made a state-by-state comparison of certain socio-economic and law enforcement factors in five clusters of states, in each of which at least one was abolitionist.[16] The data for two of the clusters, chosen at random, are reproduced in Table 10.8. They pertain to the year 1960 and the homicide rates used by the authors are those for willful homicides drawn from *Uniform Crime Reports*. The

---

16. David C. Baldus and James W. L. Cole, "A Comparison of the Work of Thorsten Sellin and Isaac Ehrlich on the Deterrent Effect of Capital Punishment," *Yale Law Journal,* vol. 85, 1975, pp. 170-186.

Table 10.8: Comparative Socioeconomic and Law Enforcement Data for Two Groups of States, 1960

	Michigan*	Indiana	Ohio	Rhode* Island	Massachusetts	Connecticut
Homicide rate per 100,000 population	4.5	4.3	3.2	1.0	1.6	
Labor force participation (%)	54.9	55.3	54.9	55.6	56.5	58.3
Unemployment rate (%)	6.9	4.2	5.5	5.3	4.2	4.6
Population aged 15-24 (%)	12.9	13.4	12.9	13.7	12.7	12.1
Real per capita income ($)	1292	1176	1278	1194	1309	1542
Nonwhite population (%)	10.4	6.4	9.8	2.5	2.5	4.6
Per capita government expenditure, state and local ($)	363	289	338	296	355	347
Per capita police expenditure, state and local ($)	11.3	7.6	9.0	10.8	12.9	11.8

SOURCE: Baldus and Cole, *op. cit.*, Table III.
NOTE: Probability of apprehension and conviction rates given in the table are omitted; they were described as unreliable because based on small and nonrandom samples.

*Abolition state.

authors conclude that the differences in the factors "among the states in each group are generally small and, more importantly, that they do not explain the differences in the observed homicide rates."[17]

Bailey undertook a similar test based on data on persons convicted of first-degree or second degree murder and committed to state penal institutions in 1967 and 1968 in 42 states. The information gathered permitted him to compute commitment rates for the two degrees of murder, separately and combined, for each of the two years, and compare them with the rates of willful homicide. To meet the objection that simple comparisons of the rates of contiguous abolitionist and retentionist states can yield no meaningful conclusion on the matter of deterrence because they "are not similar enough," Bailey compared the rates "for death penalty and abolition jurisdictions that are similar on two socioeconomic and five demographic factors: 1. median family income, 2. median education, 3. per cent non-white, 4. per cent population 18-44 years, 5. population, 6. population density, 7. per cent population residing in metropolitan areas."[18] The result of his analysis "revealed that...for both years at all levels on the control variables (with but one exception) rates are higher in capital punishment states."[19]

A reference was made in Chapter 8 to the econometric study of the deterrent effect of capital punishment published in 1975 by Isaac Ehrlich. Its claim that a capital execution would indeed deter some potential killers and perhaps save as many as eight lives was eagerly cited by retributionists, and the sophisticated multivariate regression analysis upon which the claim was based was praised as vastly superior to the simple analyses used in earlier studies, which were characterized

---

17. *Ibid.*, p. 177, fn. 30.
18. William C. Bailey, "Murder and Capital Punishment: Some Further Evidence," in Hugo Adam Bedau and Chester M. Pierce, eds., *Capital Punishment in the United States* (New York: AMS Press, 1976), pp. 314-335, p. 324.
19. *Ibid.*, p. 331.

as "extremely primitive statistically" and their authors as "not very good statisticians."[20] The claim seemed so outrageously at odds with the findings of earlier studies in the United States and abroad, going back a century and a half, that it proved a challenge to other competent statisticians and *economists*, who proceeded to subject it to tests and replications. The results are enlightening.

Passell and Taylor, after reexamining Ehrlich's statistical methods, concluded that

> the technical approach and available data employed by Ehrlich do not permit any inference whatsoever about the deterrent effect of the death penalty.... . This does not mean that models inspired by economic theory or modern methods of statistical inference have no role to play in analyzing the causes and remedies for criminal activity. Answers to many specific questions, however, must await superior data which allow more conclusive hypothesis-testing.[21]

In a report prepared for the National Research Council, in which Ehrlich's research was evaluated, Klein, Forst, and Filatov stated that

> it seems unthinkable to us to base decisions on the use of the death penalty on Ehrlich's findings, as the Solicitor General of the United States has urged (Bork et al., 1974, pp. 32-39). They simply are not sufficiently powerful, robust or tested at this stage to warrant use in such an important case.... . The deterrent effect of capital punishment is definitely not a settled matter, and this is the strongest social scientific conclusion that can be reached at the present time.[22]

20. Gordon Tullock, "Does Punishment Deter Crime?" *The Public Interest,* vol. 36, Summer 1974, p. 103.
21. Peter Passell and John B. Taylor, "The Deterrence Controversy: a Reconsideration of the Time-Series Evidence," in Bedau and Pierce, *op. cit.,* pp. 359, 368.
22. Lawrence R. Klein, Brian Forst, and Victor Filatov, "The Deterrent Effect of Capital Punishment: an Assessment of the Estimates," in Alfred Blumstein, Jacqueline Cohen, and Daniel Nagin, eds., *Deterrence and Incapacitation: Estimating the Effects of Criminal Sanctions on Crime Rates* (Washington, DC: National Academy of Sciences, 1978), pp. 358-359.

Concentrating on data for the 1960s, which figures prominently in Ehrlich's research covering 1933-1969, Brian Forst investigated empirically the deterrent effect of capital punishment. His

> analysis differs from previous ones, both because it focusses on a unique decade during which the homicide rate increased by over 50 percent and the use of capital punishment ceased, and because it examines changes in homicides and executions over time and across states. The findings do not support the hypothesis that capital punishment deters homicides.... . Capital punishment may be a justly deserved and appropriate sanction in some instances. It is certainly an effective way to assure that a person convicted of murder will not commit further crimes. The results of this analysis suggest, however, that it is erroneous to view capital punishment as a means of reducing the homicide rate.[23]

After a thorough review of the evidence, Hans Zeisel concluded as follows:

> The evidence on whether the threat of the death penalty has a deterrent effect... is overwhelmingly on one side. None of the efforts to sharpen the measurement yardstick by replacing the overall homicide rate through more sensitive measures succeeded in discovering a deterrent effect. Nor did any effort to sharpen the analytical instruments of analysis help. Even

---

23. Brian E. Forst, "The Deterrent Effect of Capital Punishment: a Cross-State Analysis of the 1960s," *Minnesota Law Review,* vol. 61, May 1977, pp. 761-762, 764. Among others who have found Ehrlich's claim unsubstantiated, see Baldus and Cole, *op. cit,;* William J. Bowers and Glenn L. Pierce, "The Illusion of Deterrence in Isaac Ehrlich's Research on Capital Punishment," in Bedau and Pierce, *op. cit.,* pp. 372-395 (for Ehrlich's reply, see his "Deterrence: Evidence and Inference," *Yale Law Journal,* vol. 85, 1975, pp. 209-227); and Robert G. Hann, *Deterrence and the Death Penalty, a Critical Review of the Research of Isaac Ehrlich* (Ottawa: Research Division of the Solicitor General of Canada, March 1976).

regression analysis, the most sophisticated of these instruments, after careful application by the scholarly community failed to detect a deterrent effect. This then is the proper summary of the evidence on the deterrent effect of the death penalty. If there is one, it can only be minute, since not one of the many research approaches — from the simplest to the most sophisticated — was able to find it. The proper question, therefore, is whether an effect that is at best so small that no one has been able to detect it, justifies the awesome moral costs of the death penalty.[24]

Passell struck the final chord: "It cannot be proven that executions do not serve as a deterrent to murder. Proof is simply beyond the capacities of empirical social science."[25] Which reminds me of the unicorn. "It is impossible to prove that there are no unicorns. All that we can prove is that we've found none so far. If the end result of a long argument (the 'bottom line' if you prefer) is nothing more than a statement that a particular theory can't be disproved, you are probably safe in putting it in the same class as unicorns."[26] And this seems to be where the theory of the deterrent power of capital punishment belongs. Our reluctance to dispose of it in this manner is that we need it to cloak our primitive desire to see the murderer pay for his crime with his life. "It is the belief in retributive justice that makes the death penalty attractive, *especially when clothed in a functional rationalization*,"[27] i.e., in an irrational belief that it serves as the ultimate deterrent even though that can never be proved.

Considering the situation in the United States today, an indifferent observer would probably conclude that the writing

24. Hans Zeisel, "The Deterrent Effect of the Death Penalty: Facts v. Faith," in Phillip B. Kurland, ed., *The Supreme COurt Review, 1976* (Chicago: University of Chicago Press, 1977), pp. 337-338.
25. Peter Passell, "The Deterrent Effect of the Death Penalty: a Statistical Test," in Bedau and Pierce, *op. cit.*, p. 410.
26. James S. Trefil, "A Consumer's Guide to Pseudoscience," *Saturday Review*, vol. 5, April 28, 1978, p. 21.
27. Zeisel, *loc. cit.*, (emphasis added).

of tracts defending or denouncing capital punishment is a
futile exercise, since it is evident that we have decided, no
matter how haltingly, to join other civilized nations who have
abandoned the death penalty.[28] What other interpretation can
be made of the fact that since our Supreme Court in 1976 approved the use of capital punishment 549 prisoners with
sentences to death have been committed to our penal institutions prior to 1979, of whom 3 have been executed, 1 early in
1977 in Utah, 1 in Florida and 1 in Nevada in 1979? The
Florida example is particularly illustrative, because the
statute authorizing the execution, upheld by the U.S.
Supreme Court, July 2, 1976 (*Profitt* v. *Florida*), was actually
adopted in December 1972. Since then, and to the end of
1978, the number of prisoners convicted of capital murder in
Florida, sentenced to death, and committed to the state's
prisons total 149; of these 121 were still under sentence of
death at the beginning of 1979.

---

28. The latest to do so is Spain, whose new Constitution took effect December 29,
1978. Its Article 15 reads: "All have a right to life and to physical and moral integri-
ty; in no case can they be subjected to torture or to degrading punishments or treatment. The death penalty remains abolished, except for possible provisions in the
military penal code during war time."

INDEX

ABOUT THE AUTHOR

THORSTEN SELLIN is Emeritus Professor of Sociology, University of Pennsylvania, where he received his doctorate and an assistant professorship in 1922. He has been secretary general of the international Penal and Penitentiary Commission, president of the International Society of Criminology and the International Penal and Penitentiary Foundation, and chairman of several expert committees — United Nations, the Board of Trustees of Philadelphia Prisons, and the Philadelphia Police Advisory Board, the first in the nation. As member of advisory committees of the American Law Institute, he assisted in the preparation of the Youth Correction Act and the Model Penal Code, and, at the request of the National Conference of Commissioners of Uniform State Laws, he drafted its Uniform Criminal Statistics Act. He has received several awards and decorations, American and foreign, holds honorary degrees from several American and foreign universities, is an elected member of the American Philosophical Society, the Royal Society of Humanistic Knowledge (Lund), the Society of Legal History (Paris), and the Institute of Sociology (Rome), and is author of numerous articles and books, including studies of capital punishment commissioned by the American law Institute and the British Royal Commission on Capital Punishment. During 1929-1968 he was editor of *The Annals of the American Academy of Political and Social Science.*